D1326711

ANIMALS ARE AMAZING

WHALES

BY KATE RIGGS

W
FRANKLIN WATTS
LONDON•SYDNEY

Franklin Watts
First published in Great Britain in 2015 by
The Watts Publishing Group

Credits
Series Designer: The Design Lab
Production by Chelsey Luther
Art Direction: Rita Marshall
Picture Credits: Photographs by Dreamstime (Mandimiles, Outdoorsman, Joanne Weston), Getty Images (Flip Nicklin), iStockphoto (Jo Ann Crebbin, Dale Walsh), Shutterstock (CampCrazy Photography, Phillip Dyhr Hobbs, TsuneoMP), SuperStock (NHPA, Minden Pictures, Pacific Stock-Design Pics, Stock Connection)

Every attempt has been made to clear copyright. Should there be any inadvertent omission please apply to the publisher for rectification.

Dewey number: 599.5
HB ISBN: 978 1 4451 4515 0

Printed in China

MIX
Paper from responsible sources
FSC® C104740

Franklin Watts
An imprint of
Hachette Children's Group
Part of The Watts Publishing Group
Carmelite House
50 Victoria Embankment
London EC4Y 0DZ

An Hachette UK Company
www.hachette.co.uk

www.franklinwatts.co.uk

CONTENTS

What are whales?

A whale is an ocean **mammal**. There are two types of whale: toothed whales and baleen whales. There are 26 **species** of toothed whale. These whales have teeth. There are 13 species of baleen whale. These whales do not have teeth.

Humpback whales are a type of baleen whale.

mammal an animal that has warm blood, a backbone, breathes air and drinks milk from its mother when it is a baby.
species different types of an animal that share the same name.

5
WHALES

Whale skin

Beluga whales are toothed whales with pure white skin.

Whales have long bodies. This helps them to swim well. Their bodies are covered with smooth skin. Most whale skin is a dark colour, such as black, brown, blue or grey. Killer whales are black with white patches.

Minke whales are baleen whales. They have long, slim bodies and dark grey skin.

Enormous whales!

Whales are some of the biggest animals in the world. The blue whale is a baleen whale and is the largest whale of all. It can grow up to 30 metres long and weigh up to 180 tonnes! The smallest whale is a toothed whale called a dwarf sperm whale. It can grow up to 2.7 metres long.

The blue whale is the biggest animal that has ever lived on Earth.

Swimming whales

Whales are found in every ocean on Earth. They swim by moving their tails and flippers. A whale's tail has two flat pads at the end. These pads are called flukes. The fin whale is one of the fastest whales. It can swim at speeds of up to 40 kilometres per hour!

A whale's flukes are the last thing you'll see when it dives under the water.

Whale food

Baleen whales eat small ocean animals, fish, and **plankton**. The baleen plates inside a whale's mouth are made of stiff **bristles** that look like a comb. The baleen traps food in the whale's mouth. Toothed whales feed on larger **prey**. They eat fish, squid and even seals.

Baleen is made of the same material as your fingernails!

plankton tiny water plants and animals.
bristles short, stiff hairs.
prey animals that are killed and eaten by other animals.

New whales

Whales spray water into the air when they breathe out through their **blowholes**.

A female whale gives birth to one **calf** at a time. The calf is born in the water. Its mother helps it swim to the surface to breathe air. Whales breathe through their blowholes. A calf stays with its mother and feeds on her milk for up to three years.

blowholes the one or two holes in the top of a whale's head that open when the whale breathes in and out.
calf a baby whale.

Whale life

Some whales mostly live alone. Other whales live in groups called pods. Toothed whales click, whistle, squeak and groan to 'talk' to each other. Baleen whales can also make singing sounds. Different whales live for different lengths of time. Some whales can live for more than 100 years in the wild.

Humpback whales are well-known for their 'whale song' – the singing sounds they make.

Playful whales

Whales like to leap out of the water and splash back down – this is called breaching. Scientists think they sometimes do this just for fun! A whale can poke its head out of the water to look around. This is called spyhopping.

Spyhopping whales can stay upright for several minutes.

Whales and people

People go on special boat trips to watch whales. Often whales can be seen in big pods. They may be feeding or **migrating**. It is fun to watch these big animals leap, swim and dive!

Breaching whales splash lots of water everywhere!

migrating moving from one place to another at different times of the year.

A whale story

Why is the bond between humans and whales so strong? The Maori people of New Zealand tell a story about this. Once there was a man named Paikea. Paikea's brother was jealous of him and tried to drown him at sea. But a humpback whale saved Paikea and took him to New Zealand. There Paikea became a great leader. Later, Maori people rode whales to show they could be strong leaders too.

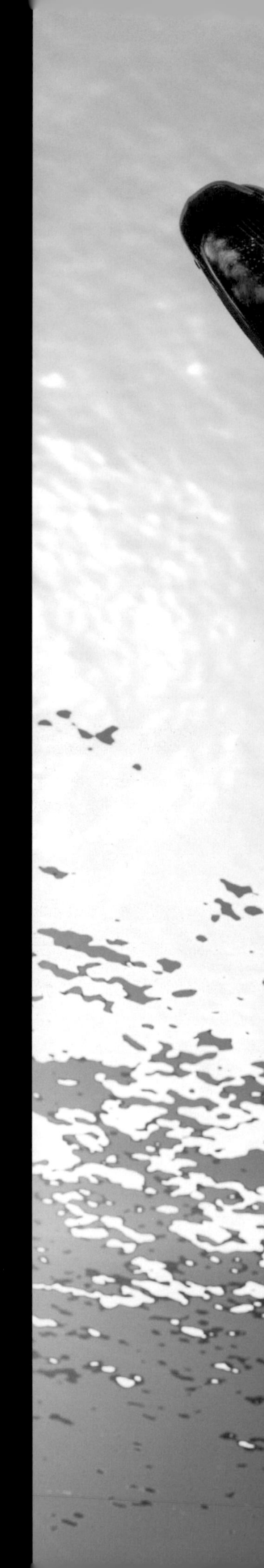

Useful information

Read More

Watery Worlds: The Open Ocean & Polar Seas by Jinny Johnson (Franklin Watts, 2015)

Wonderwise: Is a Blue Whale the Biggest Thing There Is?: A book about size by Robert E Wells (Franklin Watts, 2014)

Websites

www.dltk-kids.com/animals/whales.htm
This site has whale crafts to make and pictures of whales to colour or trace.

http://animals.nationalgeographic.com/animals/blue-whale-interactive/
This site has a feature that lets you compare the size of a blue whale with other animals and objects, such as a bus or a space shuttle.

Every effort has been made by the Publishers to ensure that these websites are suitable for children, that they are of the highest educational value and that they contain no inappropriate or offensive material. However, because of the nature of the Internet, it is impossible to guarantee that the contents of these sites will not be altered. We strongly advise that Internet access is supervised by a responsible adult.

Index

Contents

Roman Numerals

How It Works

Numbers can be written using Roman numerals.

C = 100 L = 50 X = 10 V = 5 I = 1

The same numerals next to each other are added. II = 1 + 1 = 2

Small numerals after big ones are added. LV = 50 + 5 = 55

Small numerals before big ones are subtracted. XL = 50 – 10 = 40

Some numbers can be more complicated. XCIV = 100 – 10 + 5 – 1 = 94

Now Try These

1. Circle the number shown by each Roman numeral.

8 12 22

2 8 13

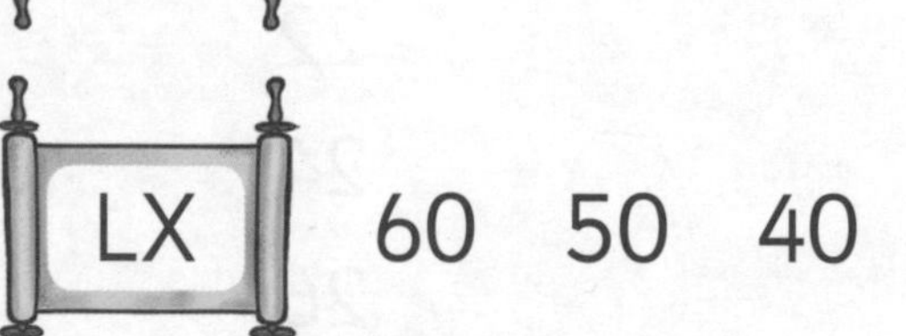

60 50 40

44 54 56

2. Write these Roman numerals as numbers.

XX = ... VI = ... XVIII = ...

LII = ... LXI = ... XXXV = ...

3. Write these Roman numerals as numbers.

  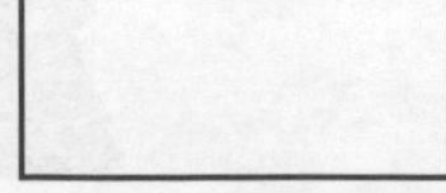 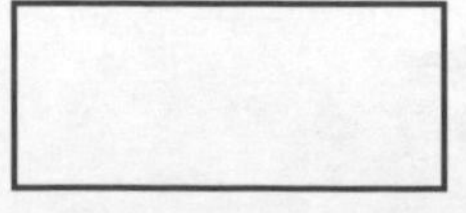 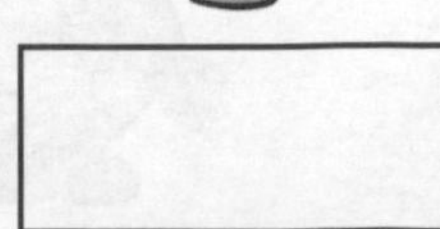

3. Circle the smallest number in each cloud.

2.3 2.1 3.2
1.9 3.0 2.5

4.2 4.3 4.5
4.9 4.1 4.0

1.12 2.16 1.23
1.06 1.14 1.02

4. Lisa's decimals have been blown out of order.
Put them back in order from smallest to largest.

3.81 3.28 3.12 3.23 3.80

5. Sandeep has recorded the length of four butterflies:

Patriot: 4.13 cm Monarch: 3.39 cm Emperor: 4.31 cm Keith: 4.03 cm

Write their names in order from longest to shortest length.

6. Put these decimals in order from largest to smallest.

1.01 0.95
1.91 2.30 ....

An Extra Challenge

Gaz has measured his height. He is 1.38 metres tall. He says, "I've grown by 2 tenths of a metre since the last time I measured."

a) How tall was Gaz the last time he measured?

b) When he takes off his shoes, he is 3 hundredths of a metre shorter. How tall is Gaz without his shoes?

How was that? Have you put decimals in their place?

Written Addition

How It Works

One way to make adding big numbers simpler is to write the sum in columns.

Here's an example: 2645 + 3182 = ?

1. Line up the numbers in place value columns.
2. Add the numbers in each column from right to left.
3. If the answer is more than 9, carry the left-hand digit to the next column. E.g. 4 + 8 = 12

```
  2 6 4 5
+ 3 1 8 2
  5 8 2 7
      1
```

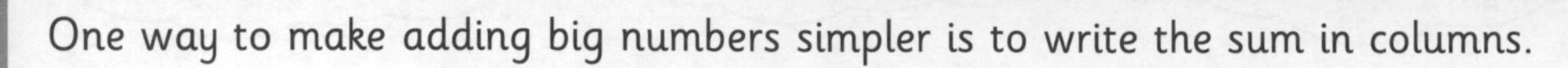

You can add decimals in the same way too. Just line up the decimal points.

Now Try These

1. Use the column method to answer these sums.

```
  2 1 9        1 2 4        2 5 3
+   6 2      + 6 1 5      + 5 6 4
```

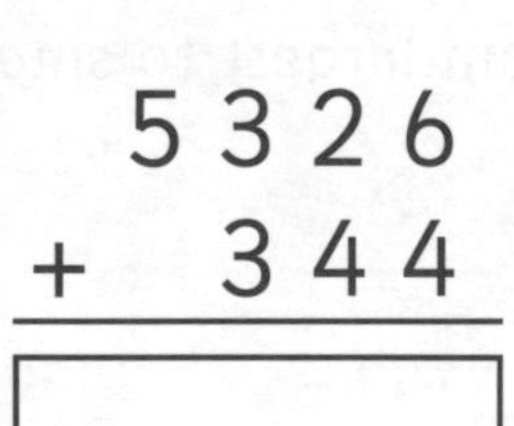

```
  3 7 1 6      5 3 2 6      7 5 5 9
+     4 8    +   3 4 4    + 1 0 6 4
```

2. Misa walks 1348 m to school and then 645 m to the park.
How far does she walk in total? Use the column method.

1348 m

645 m

Total distance:

\+

m

3. On her walk to the park, Misa finds a lost piece of homework.

   Use written addition to complete the sum.

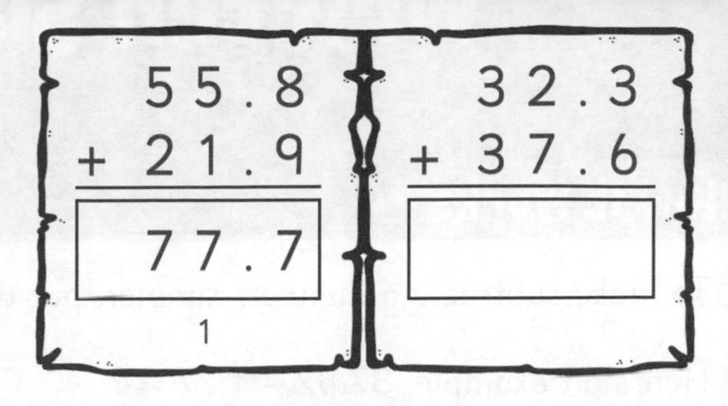

4. A funfair is open at the park.

   Leonard pays £2.45 to enter and then £1.29 to ride on the dodgems.

   Work out how much he paid in total.

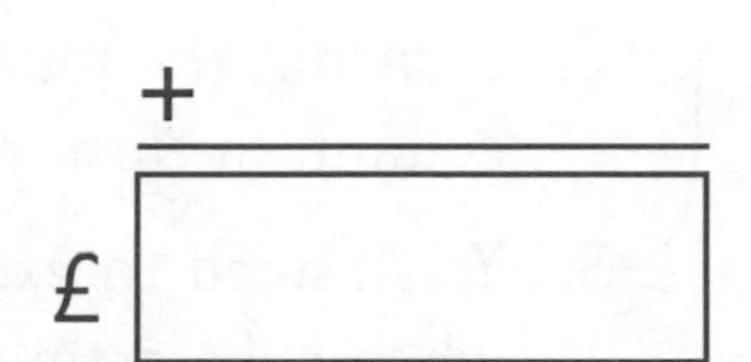

5. a) Safia buys 24.7 g of candy floss and 72.4 g of popcorn.

   How much do these snacks weigh in total?

   b) Nabil drinks 268.5 ml of pop and then 323.7 ml of water.

   How much liquid did he drink in total?

\+

g

\+

ml

An Extra Challenge

Here's some more of the homework that Misa found in Question 4.

There's some mud covering parts of the sums.

Can you work out what the covered numbers must be?

How did it go? Is everything adding up for you?

Written Subtraction

How It Works

To make subtracting numbers simpler, put them into columns.

Here's an example: 37.62 – 1.27 = ?

$$\begin{array}{r} \,^{5}\,^{12} \\ 37.\not{6}\not{2} \\ -\;\;1.27 \\ \hline 36.35 \\ \hline \end{array}$$

1. Line up the numbers in place value columns. For decimals, you line up the decimal points.
2. Subtract the numbers in each column in turn, from right to left.
3. You'll need to exchange from the next place value column when subtracting a bigger number from a smaller number.

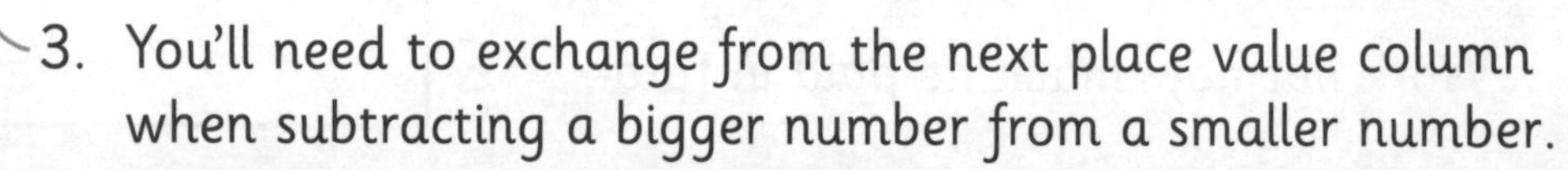

Now Try These

1. Use the column method to answer these subtractions.

$$\begin{array}{r} 4758 \\ -\;\;231 \\ \hline \end{array} \qquad \begin{array}{r} 5895 \\ -\;4621 \\ \hline \end{array} \qquad \begin{array}{r} 6782 \\ -\;\;866 \\ \hline \end{array}$$

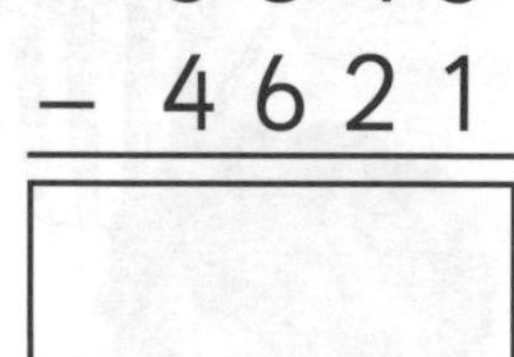

2. There are 4131 strawberries in a field. Jen picks 107 strawberries.

   How many strawberries are left in the field?

3. A bakery has sold 9542 loaves of bread and 3281 strawberry cheesecakes.

   How many **more** loaves of bread were sold than cheesecakes?

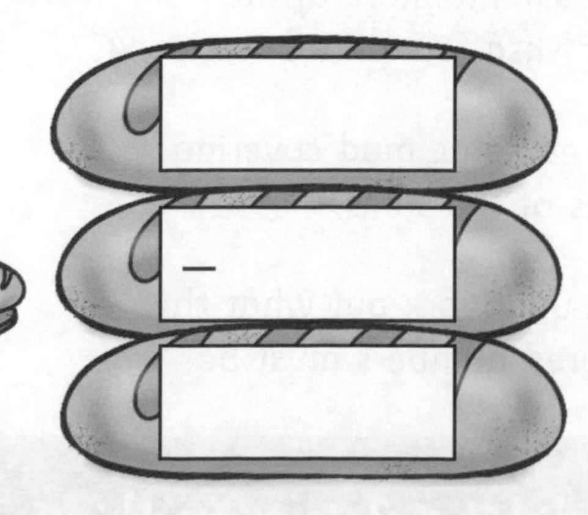

6. Use your times tables to answer these calculations.

$81 \div 9 =$ .... $28 \div 7 =$ .... $12 \div 1 =$ ....

$5 \div 5 =$ .... $22 \div 2 =$ .... $48 \div 6 =$ ....

7. Alfie throws 35 sticks for his dogs to chase.
Each dog chases 7 sticks.
How many dogs does Alfie have?

.... dogs

8. Anna has 4 pets. She cuddles each one the same number of times. She gives 48 cuddles in total.
How many cuddles does each pet get?

.... cuddles

9. Use your times tables to fill in the missing numbers.

a) $7 \times \square = 21$ b) $6 \times \square = 66$

c) $3 \times 4 \times 5 = \square$ d) $2 \times 6 \times 3 = \square$

An Extra Challenge

Here's a recipe for a witch's brew*.

a) How many cat hairs would you need to make 2 potions?

b) How much snail slime would you need to make 4 potions?

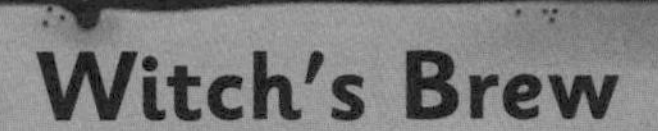

Witch's Brew

Makes <u>three</u> potions.

Cat hairs: 12

Owl feathers: 21

Snail slime: 30 ml

Cobwebs: 36

*Drinking witch's brew is not recommended for humans.

How was that? Not a cat-astrophe I hope...

Factors and Multiples

How It Works

A **multiple** of a number is what you get when you multiply that number by another whole number.

A ***factor*** of a number is another whole number that divides it exactly. Factors can be written as **factor pairs**.

$3 \times 4 = 12$ ← So 12 is a multiple of both 3 and 4.

$12 \div 3 = 4$

and

$12 \div 4 = 3$

So 3 and 4 are a factor pair of 12.

Now Try These

1. Some factors of the number in each ball are written above the cones. Draw lines to match factor pairs. One has been done for you.

2. Use division or multiplication to show why each statements is true. One has been done for you.

a) 3 is a factor of 18.

$18 \div 3 = 6$

b) 6 is a factor of 42.

....

c) 45 is a multiple of 9.

....

d) 60 is a multiple of 5.

....

3. In each goal, colour in all the multiples of the number that the coach is calling out.

Three!

27	61	8	50
11	20	31	15
12	25	4	10

Seven!

6	31	77	39
49	45	24	21
54	57	15	81

4. Which statements are correct? Put a tick (✔) or a cross (✘) next to each one.

a) 9 is a factor of 27. ☐

b) 16 is a multiple of 3. ☐

c) 4 is a factor of 34. ☐

d) 72 is a multiple of 8. 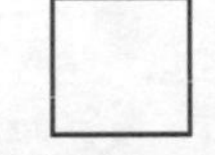

An Extra Challenge

The factors of 4 are facing the factors of 9 on the pitch below.

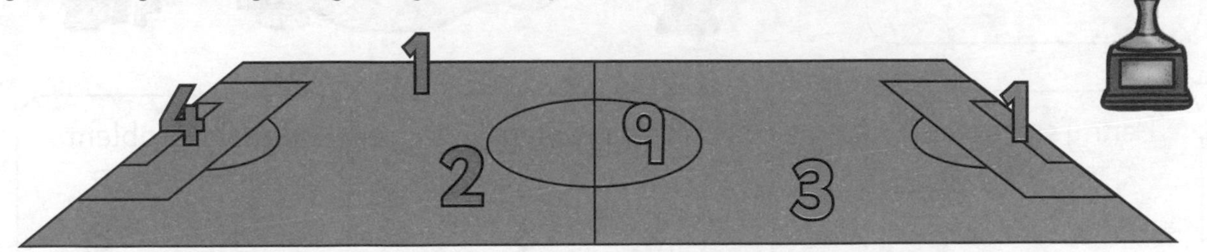

a) Use multiplication to show why both 4 and 9 are factors of 36.

b) Write down all the pairs of numbers that multiply together to give a multiple of 6.

How would you score your skills on this topic?

☐  

Written Multiplication

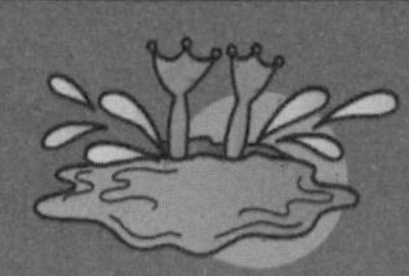

How It Works

Multiplying a 2-digit number by a 1-digit number can be done using columns. Here's an example: 23 × 5 = ?

		H	T	O
Put the big number on top and split it into tens and ones. →			2	3
	×			5
Multiply the ones... →	3 × 5 =		1	5
...and then the tens. →	20 × 5 =	1	0	0
Add them together for the answer. →	15 + 100 =	1	1	5

You can do 3-digit numbers in the same way. Just multiply the ones, tens and hundreds, then add them together.

Now Try These

1. Solve each person's multiplication problem. Then draw a line from their hook to the correct answer in the pond.

John's problem

$$\begin{array}{r} 26 \\ \times \quad 3 \\ \hline \end{array}$$

Penny's problem

$$\begin{array}{r} 32 \\ \times \quad 4 \\ \hline \end{array}$$

Osita's problem

$$\begin{array}{r} 45 \\ \times \quad 8 \\ \hline \end{array}$$

Tahel's problem

$$\begin{array}{r} 58 \\ \times \quad 8 \\ \hline \end{array}$$

2. At a pond, there are 8 times as many fish as there are ducks. There are 14 ducks.

   How many fish are there?

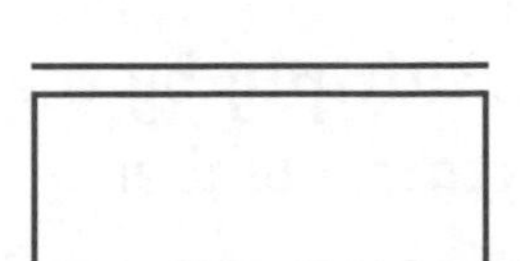

×

3. Rachael counts 36 frogs. There are 7 times as many flies as there are frogs.

   How many flies are there?

4. Solve these multiplications. Show your working. One has been done for you.

a) 350 × 4 b) 203 × 4 c) 916 × 6 d) 783 × 3

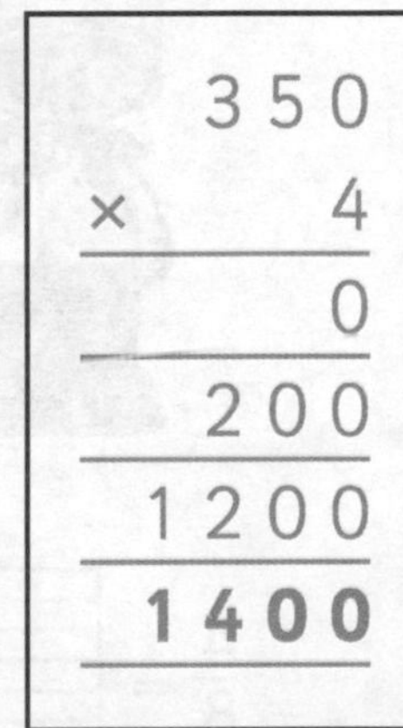

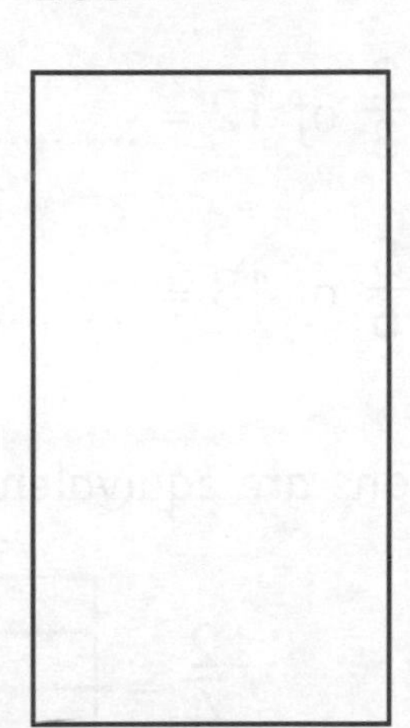

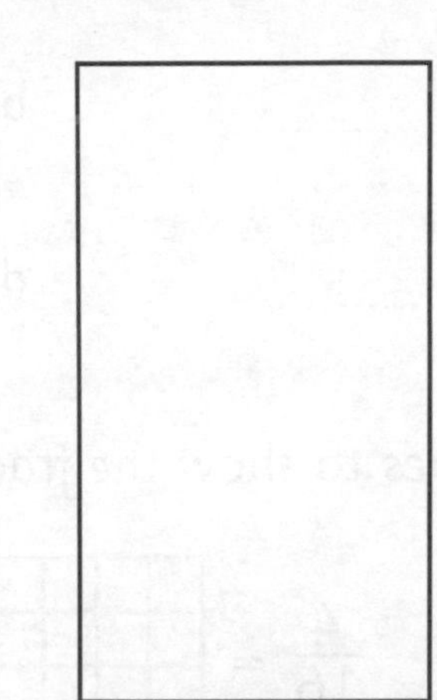

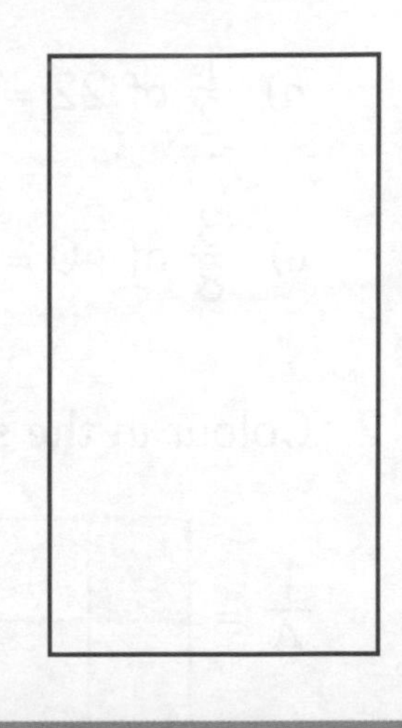

An Extra Challenge

Heath is 13 years old.

- His grandpa is 6 times as old as him.
- His house is 7 times as old as his grandpa.
- The stone monument next door is 9 times as old as his house.

How old is the stone monument?

Did you do well? If not, just hop back and try again.

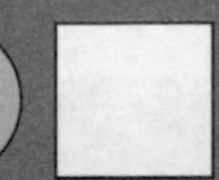

Fractions 1

How It Works

To find a fraction of an amount, just **divide** by the **bottom** number and **multiply** by the **top** number. Here's how to find $\frac{3}{4}$ of 8:

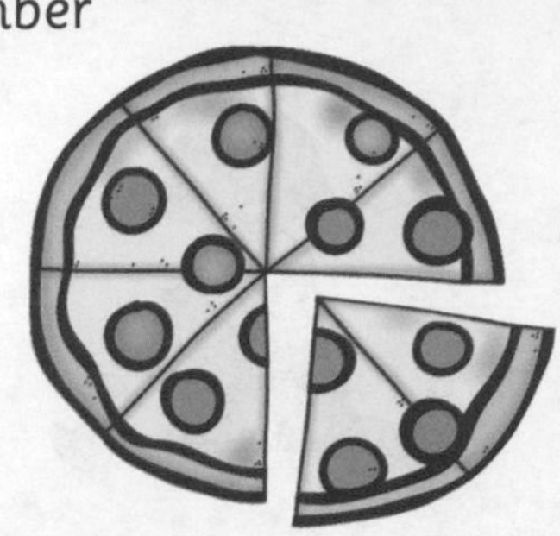

$$8 \div 4 = 2 \text{ and } 2 \times 3 = 6 \qquad \text{So } \frac{3}{4} \text{ of } 8 = 6$$

It works the other way around too. You can **multiply** by the **top** number first, and then **divide** by the **bottom** number.

Now Try These

1. Work out these fractions of amounts.

a) $\frac{1}{2}$ of 22 = ...

b) $\frac{2}{3}$ of 12 = ...

c) $\frac{3}{8}$ of 40 = ...

d) $\frac{5}{6}$ of 18 = ...

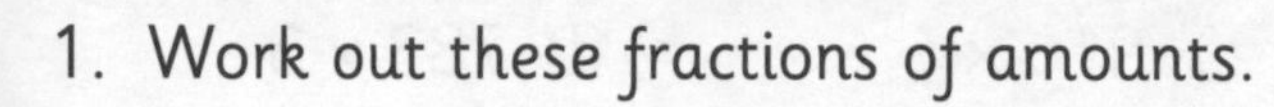

2. Colour in the shapes to show the fractions are equivalent.

$\frac{1}{4}$ = ⬜ $\frac{4}{16}$ = ⬜ $\frac{2}{4}$ = ⬜ $\frac{4}{8}$ = ⬜

$\frac{1}{3}$ = ⬜ $\frac{2}{6}$ = ⬜ $\frac{3}{4}$ = ⬜ $\frac{6}{8}$ = ⬜

3. a) There are 15 slices of pizza at a picnic. Lev eats $\frac{2}{5}$ of them.

How many slices of pizza does Lev eat?

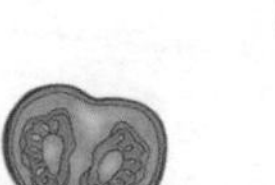

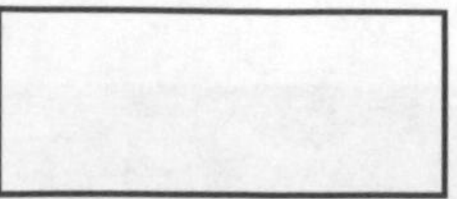

b) A pizza has 42 items on top. $\frac{4}{7}$ of the items are mushrooms slices.

How many mushrooms slices are there in total?

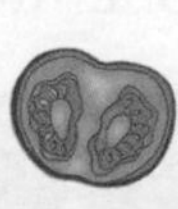

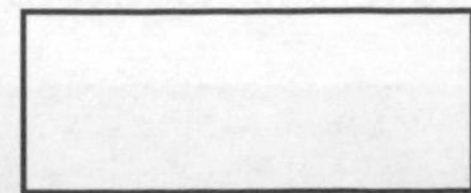

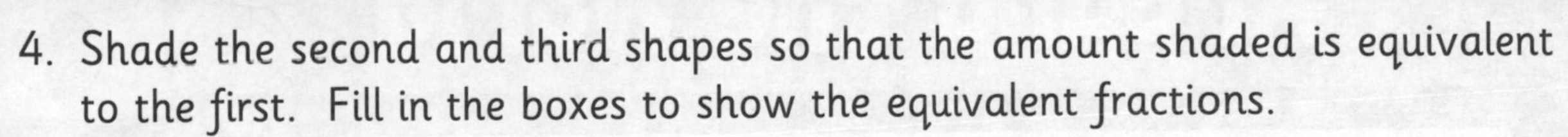

4. Shade the second and third shapes so that the amount shaded is equivalent to the first. Fill in the boxes to show the equivalent fractions.

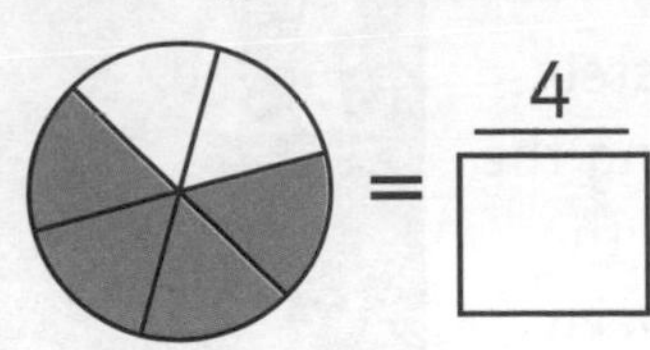

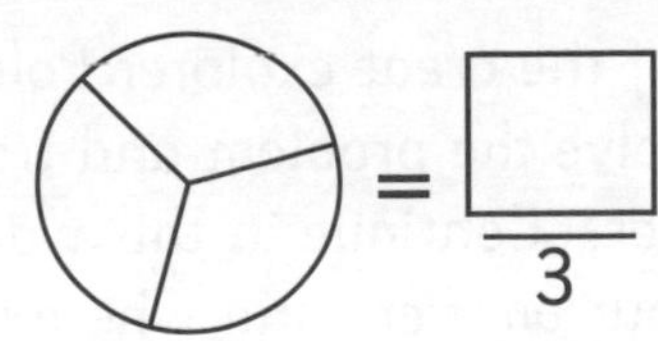

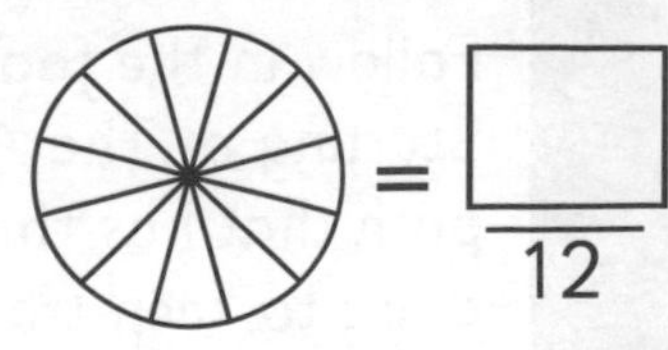

5. A tower is 56 m tall. Lacy climbs $\frac{3}{8}$ of its height.

   How high has she climbed?

.... m

6. Write down how many tenths and hundredths are shaded in each diagram.

a)

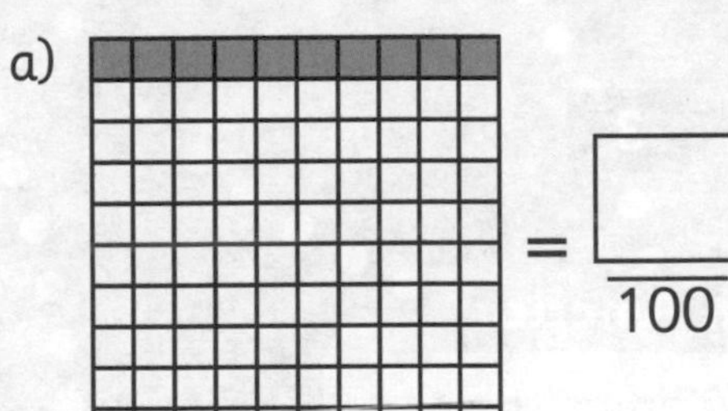

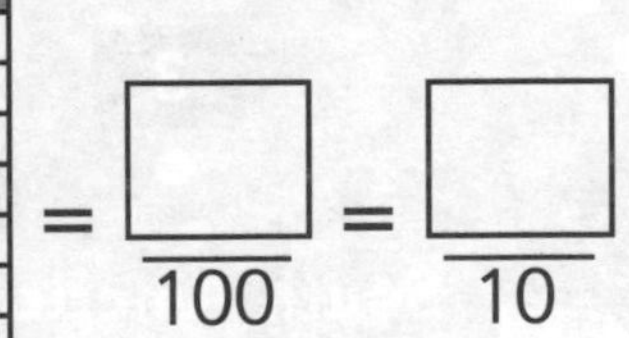

b)

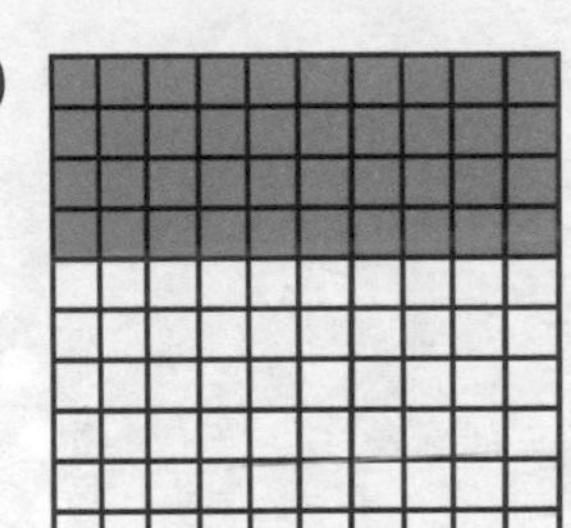

7. Gurdeep has £100. He spends $\frac{29}{100}$ of his money on food.

   How much does he spend on the food?

£ ....

An Extra Challenge

Kim has this coupon for a restaurant.

$\frac{3}{5}$ off the price of any meal

a) How much would Kim **save** on a meal that usually costs £15?

b) Leo has a coupon for $\frac{2}{3}$ off the price of any meal. Who would pay the most for the meal costing £15? Explain how you know.

Are you full up with fractions? Or are you hungry for more?

Around the World

Follow in the footsteps of the great explorer Polar Bearstein. Starting at The Arctic, solve the problem and travel along the path that has that answer. Continue in this way, using the diary to keep track of your answers and where you've been. What route did Polar Bearstein take to get around the world?

North America

When 0.75 is written as a fraction with a 4 on the bottom, what number goes on the top?

4

3

2

South America

In the 7 times table (up to 12 × 7), how many numbers are a multiple of 6?

7

16

8

5

Africa

What number is in the hundreds column of the answer to 3825 + 4957?

4

What (in cm that's 4

A

What

2. Use division or multiplication to show why each statements is true. One has been done for you.

a) 3 is a factor of 18.

18 ÷ 3 = 6

....

b) 6 is a factor of 42.

....

c) 45 is a multiple of 9.

....

d) 60 is a multiple of 5.

....

3. In each goal, colour in all the multiples of the number that the coach is calling out.

Three!

27	61	8	50
11	20	31	15
12	25	4	10

Seven!

6	31	77	39
49	45	24	21
54	57	15	81

4. Which statements are correct? Put a tick (✔) or a cross (✘) next to each one.

a) 9 is a factor of 27. ☐

b) 16 is a multiple of 3. ☐

c) 4 is a factor of 34. ☐

d) 72 is a multiple of 8. 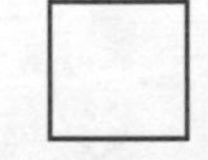

An Extra Challenge

The factors of 4 are facing the factors of 9 on the pitch below.

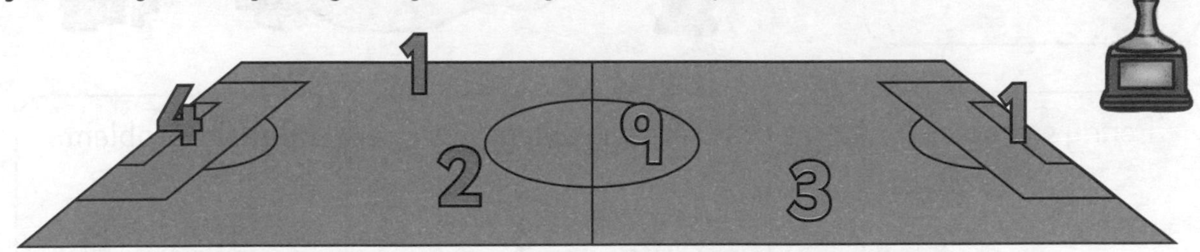

a) Use multiplication to show why both 4 and 9 are factors of 36.

b) Write down all the pairs of numbers that multiply together to give a multiple of 6.

How would you score your skills on this topic?

Written Multiplication

How It Works

Multiplying a 2-digit number by a 1-digit number can be done using columns. Here's an example: $23 \times 5 = ?$

Step		H T O
Put the big number on top and split it into tens and ones.		2 3
		× 5
Multiply the ones...	$3 \times 5 =$	1 5
...and then the tens.	$20 \times 5 =$	1 0 0
Add them together for the answer.	$15 + 100 =$	1 1 5

You can do 3-digit numbers in the same way. Just multiply the ones, tens and hundreds, then add them together.

Now Try These

1. Solve each person's multiplication problem. Then draw a line from their hook to the correct answer in the pond.

John's problem

$$\begin{array}{r} 26 \\ \times \quad 3 \\ \hline \end{array}$$

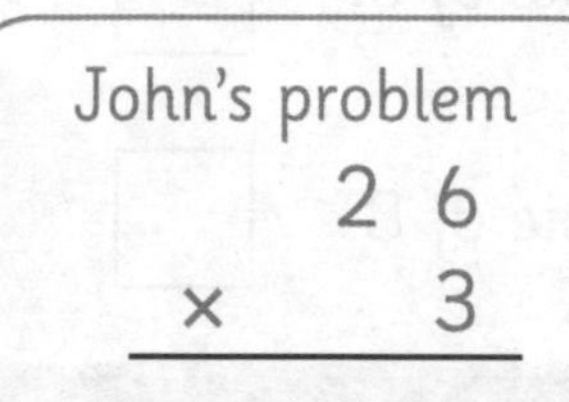

Penny's problem

$$\begin{array}{r} 32 \\ \times \quad 4 \\ \hline \end{array}$$

Osita's problem

$$\begin{array}{r} 45 \\ \times \quad 8 \\ \hline \end{array}$$

Tahel's problem

$$\begin{array}{r} 58 \\ \times \quad 8 \\ \hline \end{array}$$

2. At a pond, there are 8 times as many fish as there are ducks. There are 14 ducks.

   How many fish are there?

×

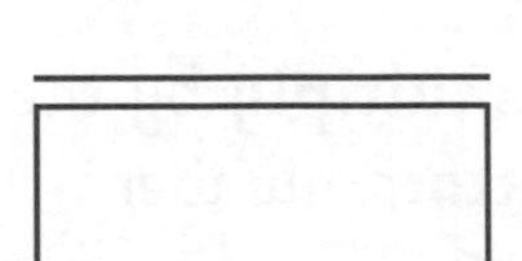

3. Rachael counts 36 frogs. There are 7 times as many flies as there are frogs.

   How many flies are there?

×

4. Solve these multiplications. Show your working. One has been done for you.

a) 350 × 4

```
  350
×   4
    0
  200
 1200
 1400
```

b) 203 × 4

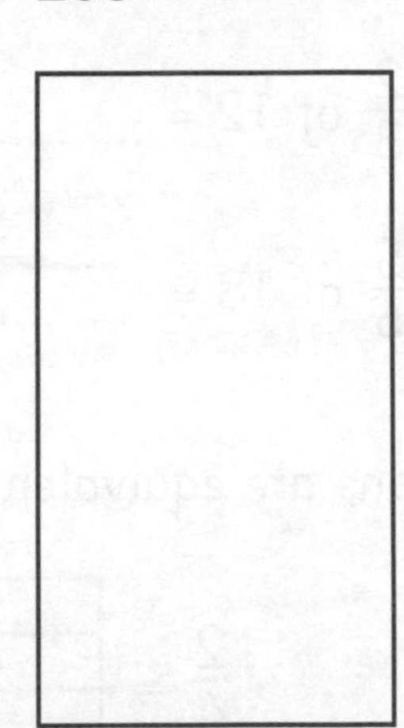

c) 916 × 6

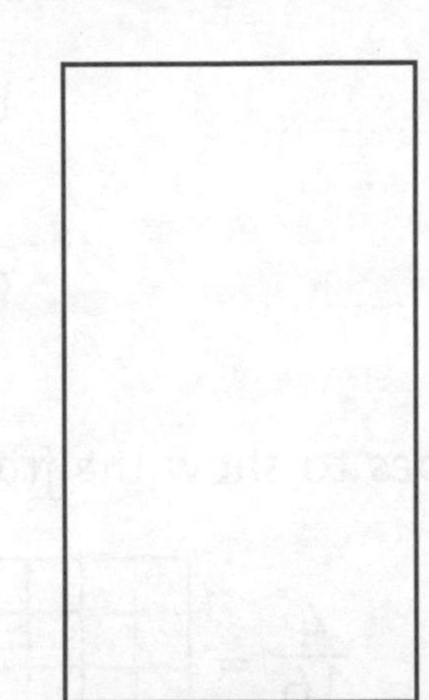

d) 783 × 3

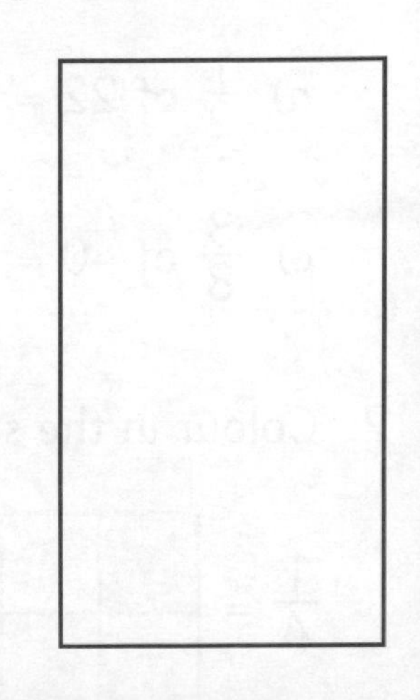

An Extra Challenge

Heath is 13 years old.

- His grandpa is 6 times as old as him.
- His house is 7 times as old as his grandpa.
- The stone monument next door is 9 times as old as his house.

How old is the stone monument?

Did you do well? If not, just hop back and try again.

Fractions 1

How It Works

To find a fraction of an amount, just **divide** by the **bottom** number and **multiply** by the **top** number. Here's how to find $\frac{3}{4}$ of 8:

$$8 \div 4 = 2 \text{ and } 2 \times 3 = 6 \qquad \text{So } \frac{3}{4} \text{ of } 8 = 6$$

It works the other way around too. You can **multiply** by the **top** number first, and then **divide** by the **bottom** number.

Now Try These

1. Work out these fractions of amounts.

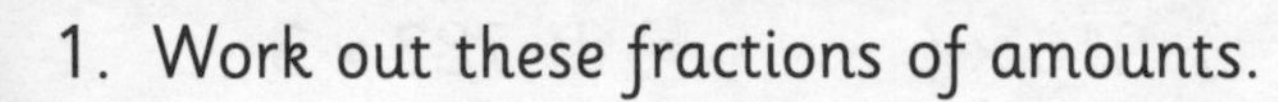

a) $\frac{1}{2}$ of 22 = ...   b) $\frac{2}{3}$ of 12 = ...

c) $\frac{3}{8}$ of 40 = ...   d) $\frac{5}{6}$ of 18 = ...

2. Colour in the shapes to show the fractions are equivalent.

$\frac{1}{4}$ = $\frac{4}{16}$ = $\frac{2}{4}$ = $\frac{4}{8}$ =

$\frac{1}{3}$ = $\frac{2}{6}$ = $\frac{3}{4}$ = $\frac{6}{8}$ =

3. a) There are 15 slices of pizza at a picnic. Lev eats $\frac{2}{5}$ of them.

How many slices of pizza does Lev eat?

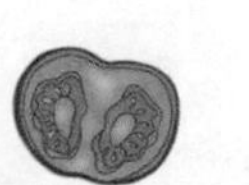

b) A pizza has 42 items on top. $\frac{4}{7}$ of the items are mushrooms slices.

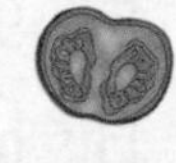

How many mushrooms slices are there in total?

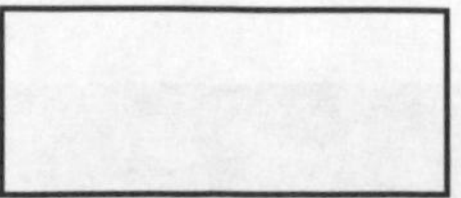

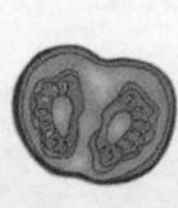

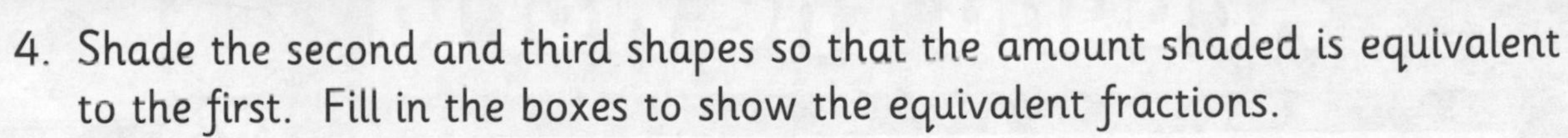

4. Shade the second and third shapes so that the amount shaded is equivalent to the first. Fill in the boxes to show the equivalent fractions.

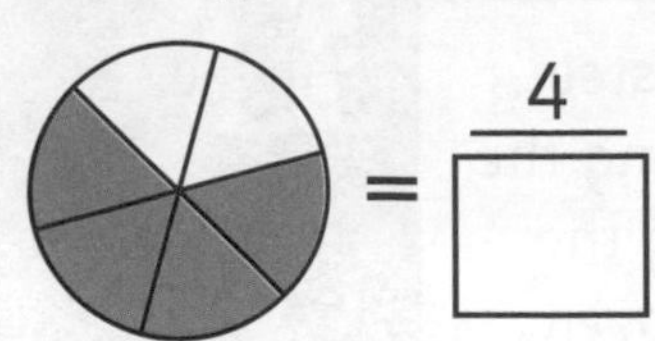

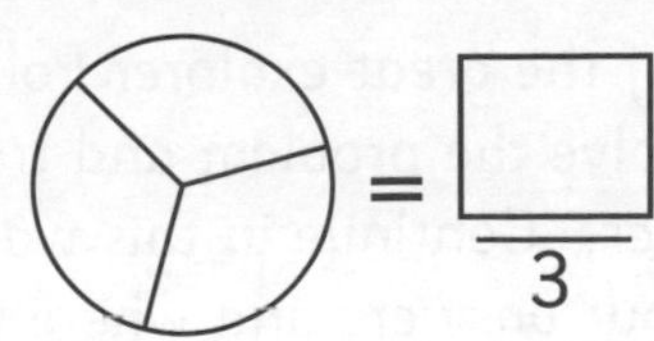

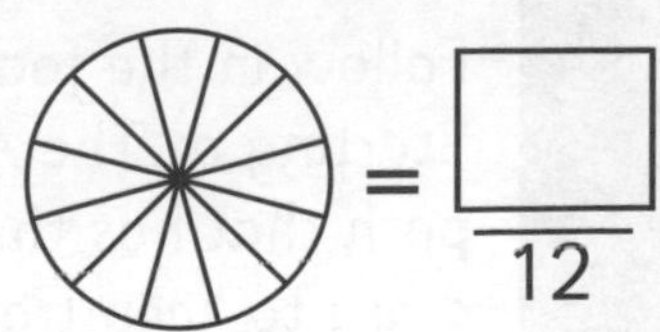

5. A tower is 56 m tall. Lacy climbs $\frac{3}{8}$ of its height.

   How high has she climbed?

   .... m

6. Write down how many tenths and hundredths are shaded in each diagram.

   a) 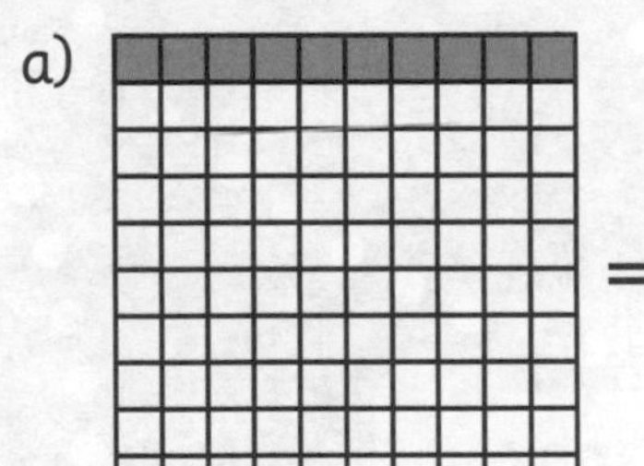 = $\frac{\square}{100}$ = $\frac{\square}{10}$

   b) 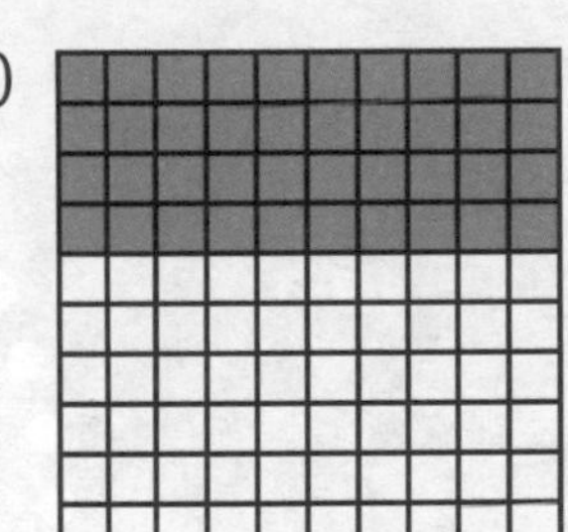 = $\frac{\square}{100}$ = $\frac{\square}{10}$

7. Gurdeep has £100. He spends $\frac{29}{100}$ of his money on food.

   How much does he spend on the food?

   £ ....

An Extra Challenge

Kim has this coupon for a restaurant.

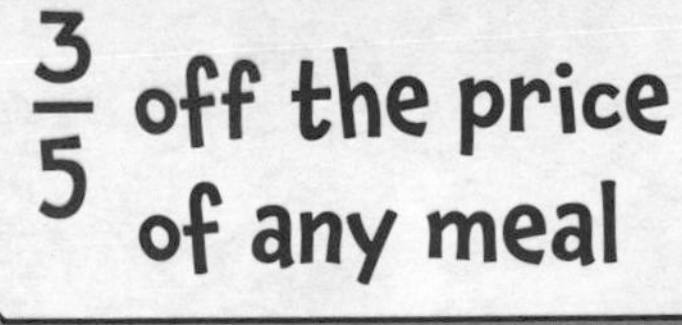

a) How much would Kim **save** on a meal that usually costs £15?

b) Leo has a coupon for $\frac{2}{3}$ off the price of any meal. Who would pay the most for the meal costing £15? Explain how you know.

Are you full up with fractions? Or are you hungry for more?

Around the World

Follow in the footsteps of the great explorer Polar Bearstein. Starting at The Arctic, solve the problem and travel along the path that has that answer. Continue in this way, using the diary to keep track of your answers and where you've been. What route did Polar Bearstein take to get around the world?

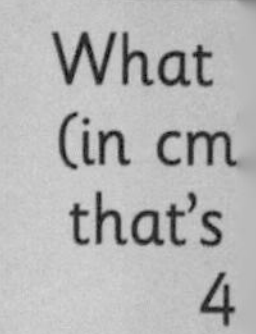

North America

When 0.75 is written as a fraction with a 4 on the bottom, what number goes on the top?

4

What
(in cm
that's
4

3

2

South America

In the 7 times table (up to 12 × 7), how many numbers are a multiple of 6?

7

16

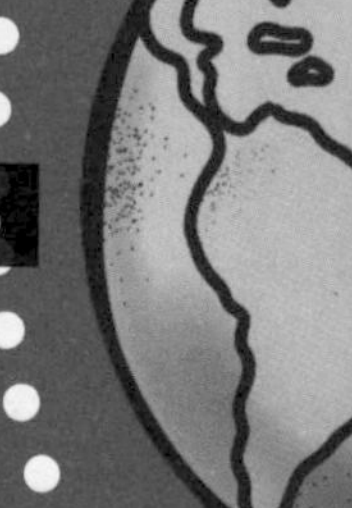

8

5

Africa

What number is in the hundreds column of the answer to 3825 + 4957?

A

4

What

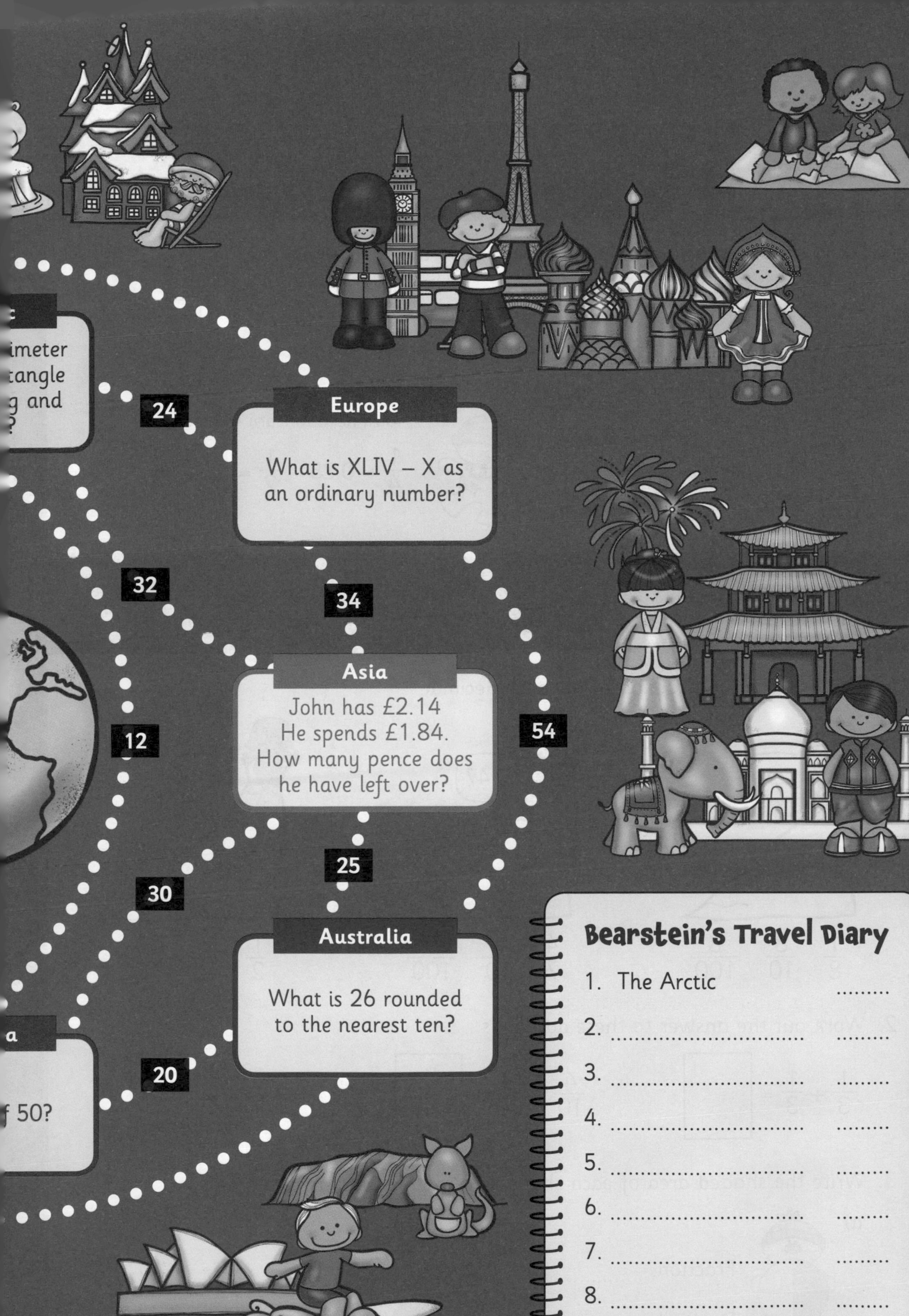
24
Europe
What is XLIV – X as an ordinary number?
32
34
Asia
John has £2.14
He spends £1.84.
How many pence does he have left over?
12
54
30
25
Australia
What is 26 rounded to the nearest ten?
20
Bearstein's Travel Diary
1. The Arctic ....
2. ....
3. ....
4. ....
5. ....
6. ....
7. ....
8. ....
9. ....

Fractions 2

How It Works

You can add and subtract fractions if they have the same denominator.

$\frac{1}{10} + \frac{3}{10} = \frac{4}{10}$ ← $1 + 3 = 4$
← The denominator stays the same.

$\frac{3}{10} - \frac{1}{10} = \frac{2}{10}$ ← $3 - 1 = 2$
← The denominator stays the same.

You can also show fractions as decimals:

$\frac{1}{10} = 0.1$ $\frac{3}{10} = 0.3$

$\frac{3}{100} = 0.03$ $\frac{59}{100} = 0.59$

You'll need to learn these ones:

$\frac{1}{4} = 0.25$ $\frac{1}{2} = 0.5$ $\frac{3}{4} = 0.75$

Now Try These

1. Circle the correct fraction below each decimal.

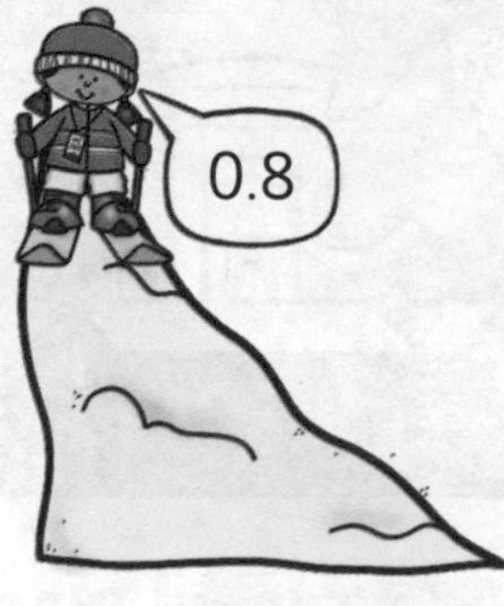

$\frac{1}{8}$ $\frac{8}{10}$ $\frac{8}{100}$

$\frac{4}{7}$ $\frac{47}{10}$ $\frac{47}{100}$

$\frac{1}{2}$ $\frac{5}{10}$ $\frac{5}{100}$

2. Work out the answer to these additions.

$\frac{1}{3} + \frac{1}{3} =$ ☐ $\frac{4}{10} + \frac{3}{10} =$ ☐ $\frac{3}{8} + \frac{4}{8} =$ ☐

3. Write the shaded area of each shape as a fraction and as a decimal.

a)

Fraction: ....

Decimal: ....

b)

Fraction: ....

Decimal: ....

4. Find the answer to each subtraction in the snowball pile below it. Show your choice by crossing out the wrong fractions.

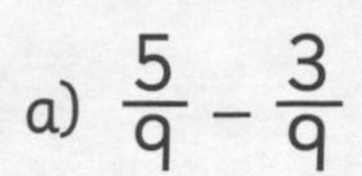
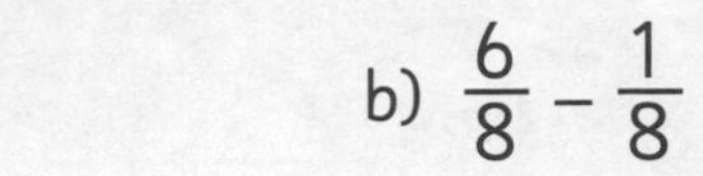

a) $\frac{5}{9} - \frac{3}{9}$ b) $\frac{6}{8} - \frac{1}{8}$ c) $\frac{8}{11} - \frac{7}{11}$

5. Write your answer to these questions in the snow people's boxes.

a) What is 0.01 as a fraction? b) What is 0.17 as a fraction?

6. Write these fractions as decimals.

$\frac{7}{10}$ = ☐ $\frac{82}{100}$ = ☐ $\frac{29}{100}$ = ☐

An Extra Challenge

Can you work out what numbers have been covered in these calculations?

$\frac{?}{10} + \frac{5}{10} = 0.9$ $\frac{3}{10} + \frac{?}{10} = 0.6$

$\frac{4}{100} - \frac{?}{100} = 0.02$ $\frac{22}{100} - \frac{?}{100} = 0.17$

How were these pages? Have you got fractions figured out?

Rounding

How It Works

You can **round** any number to the nearest whole number, 10, 100 or 1000.
You can see how this works by looking at where a number is on a number line.

Round 8.7 to the nearest whole number.

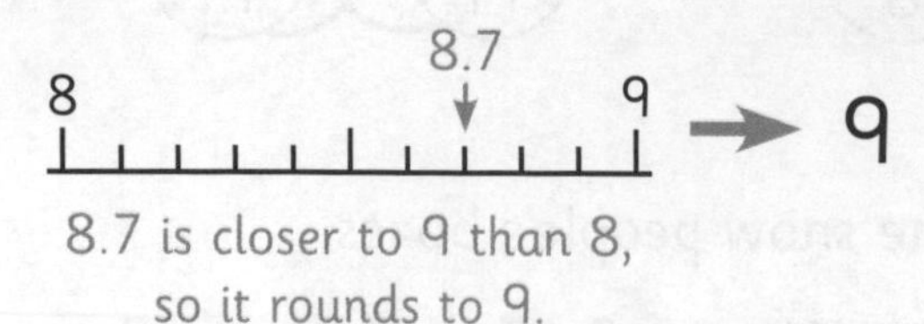

8.7 is closer to 9 than 8,
so it rounds to 9.

Round 64 to the nearest 10.

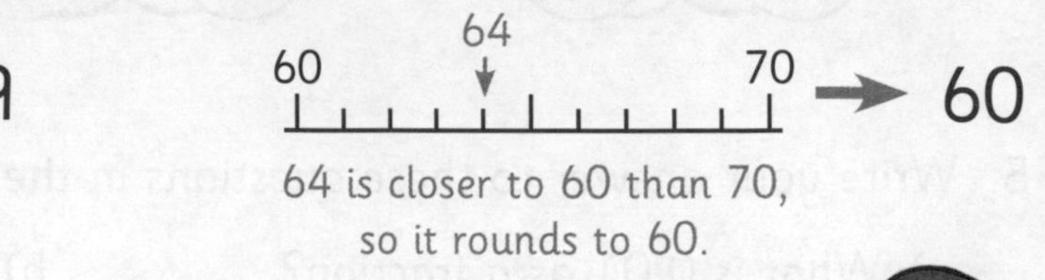

64 is closer to 60 than 70,
so it rounds to 60.

If the number you're rounding is exactly in the middle of two possible answers, then round it up to the bigger one.

Now Try These

1. Round each number to the nearest 10, 100 and 1000.

	731	1069
Nearest 10	730	
Nearest 100		
Nearest 1000		

2. Round each decimal on the ship's sails to the nearest whole number.
Write your answers on the second ship.

3. Circle the numbers that round to 330 to the nearest ten.

4. Round each number to the nearest 10 in these problems:

a) A treasure chest contains 28 gold coins and 19 gold bars. Estimate how many pieces of gold there are in total.

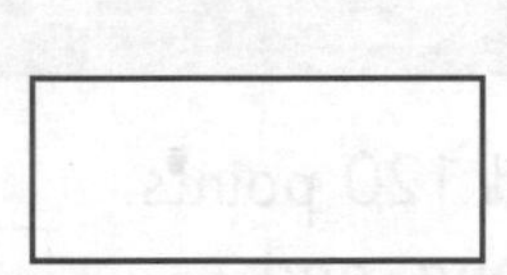

b) Pete mopped 63 decks and Sally mopped 49 decks. Estimate how many more decks Pete mopped than Sally.

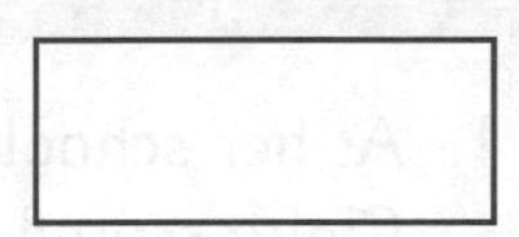

5. Estimate these calculations by rounding each decimal to the nearest whole number.

1.9 + 5.2 = ... 12.4 – 4.7 = ... 3.3 × 5.1 = ...

An Extra Challenge

Polly has been cursed. She can only say a number by rounding it to the nearest 10.

a) Is it possible that Polly has been stuck on the island for exactly 97 days?

b) What is the smallest possible number of days that Polly could have been stuck on the island?

c) What is the largest possible number of days that Polly could have been stuck on the island?

How aarrr ye getting along with rounding?

Problem Solving

How It Works

Some problems won't tell you whether you need to **add**, **subtract**, **multiply** or **divide**. You need to decide what to do. Here's an example:

Jamil's yoga class costs £4.59 but he has only £1.25. Sarah gives Jamil the money he needs. She has £2.13 left over. How much money did Sarah start with?

First work out how much money Sarah gave to Jamil.

$$\begin{array}{r} 4.59 \\ -\ 1.25 \\ \hline 3.34 \end{array}$$

£4.59 – £1.25 = £3.34
So Sarah gave Jamil £3.34.

Then add this to the amount that Sarah had left over.

$$\begin{array}{r} 2.13 \\ +\ 3.34 \\ \hline 5.47 \end{array}$$

£2.13 + £3.34 = £5.47
So Sarah started with £5.47.

Now Try These

1. At her school sports day, Winona scored 120 points. Claire scored 57 points fewer than Winona, and Abigail scored 91 points more than Claire. Fill in these results on the scorecards.

1st
Name: ....
Score: .... points

2nd
Name: ....
Score: .... points

3rd
Name: ....
Score: .... points

2. Ruth has 112 eggs. She sells 64 eggs, then her chickens lay another 37 eggs. How many eggs does she have now?

.... eggs

3. At his school sports day, Martin takes part in 9 events. He scores 14 points in each of the first 6 events and then 7 points in each of the remaining events. How many points did he score in total?

.... points

4. An athletics club has membership fee of £7 for 11-16 year olds and £5 for under 10s.

The members paid a combined total of £169. The club has 15 members that are under 10.

How many members of the club are 11-16 years old?

.... members

5. At a shop, bottles of water cost 50p each or £1.12 for a pack of 3. James has £5. He buys as many bottles as he can. How much change does he get?

.... p

An Extra Challenge

Three friends team up in a relay race. Jessica runs first, before handing over to Andy. Andy goes second and then hands over to Peter. Peter finishes the race.

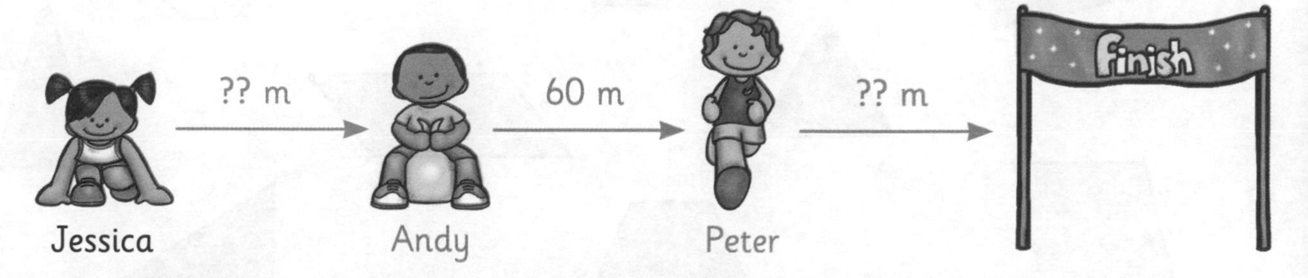

The race is 240 m long in total. Andy travels 60 m.
Jessica runs 20 m further than Peter. How far did Peter run?

How did it go? Did you get through these tricky problems?

     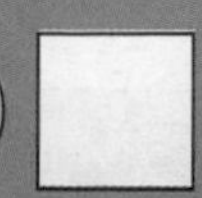

Shapes and Angles

How It Works

Angles less than a $\frac{1}{4}$ turn are **acute**.

Angles between a $\frac{1}{4}$ and $\frac{1}{2}$ turn are **obtuse**.

Shapes can be described using properties such as angles and lines of symmetry.

For example: isosceles triangles have two equal angles, two equal sides and one line of symmetry.

This angle is obtuse.

Here's the line of symmetry.

These are acute angles.

Now Try These

1. Make each sentence true by crossing out the wrong word.

   a) A triangle that has three sides of the same length is called an **equilateral / isosceles** triangle.

   b) A quadrilateral with two pairs of equal length sides and no parallel sides is called a **rhombus / kite**.

2. Draw lines to join up the shapes with their names.

regular hexagon | scalene triangle | equilateral triangle | irregular hexagon

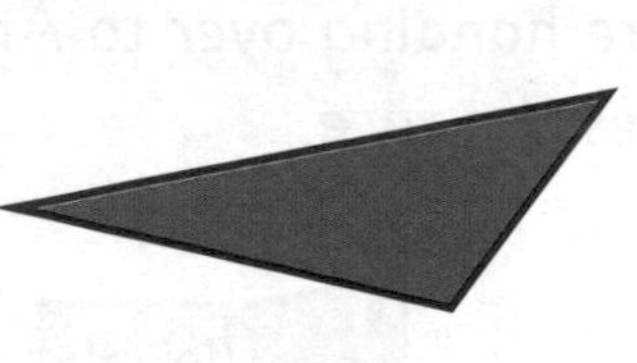

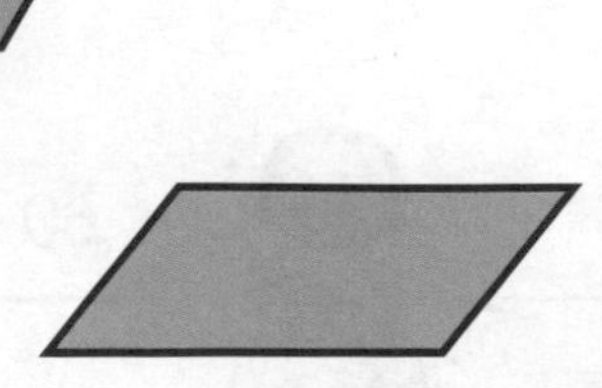

trapezium | rhombus | isosceles triangle | right-angled triangle | parallelogram

3. Fill in the empty spaces to complete this table.

Shape			
Number of sides	3		
Number of acute angles		3	
Number of obtuse angles			4
Number of lines of symmetry			

4. Complete the shapes, making them symmetrical along the dotted line.

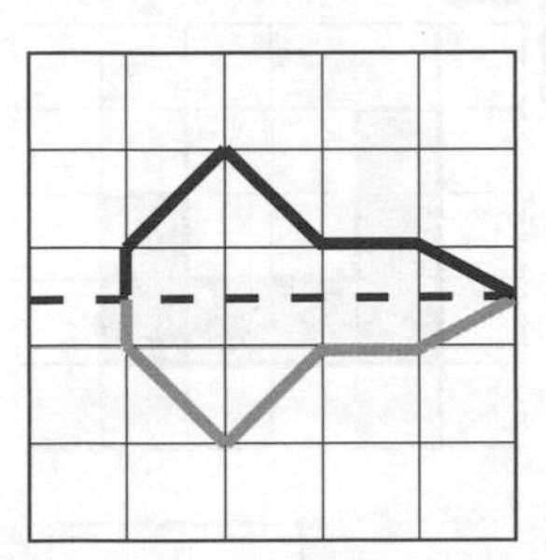

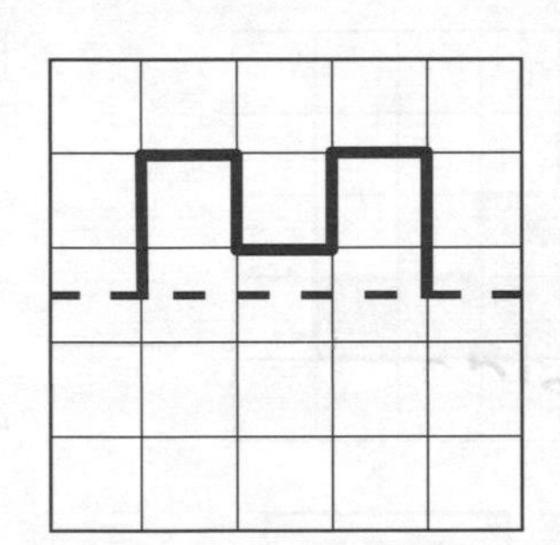

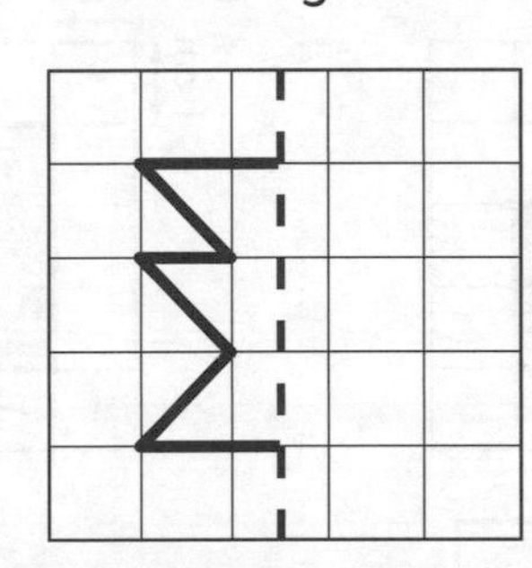

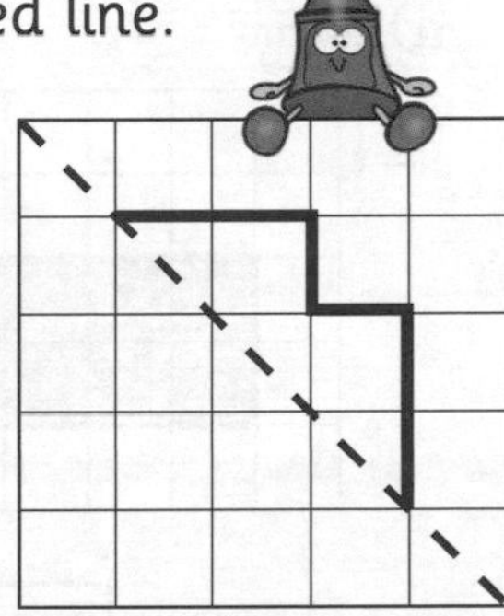

An Extra Challenge

What shapes are these children thinking about?

It has three angles. One of its angles is a quarter turn.

It has five sides of equal length. All five angles have the same size too.

It's a quadrilateral with two lines of symmetry, but no right angles.

Are you shaping up to be an expert with angles?

Perimeter and Area

How It Works

Perimeter is the distance around the outside of a shape. Find it by adding up the lengths of the sides.

Area is the space inside the shape. Work it out by counting the squares.

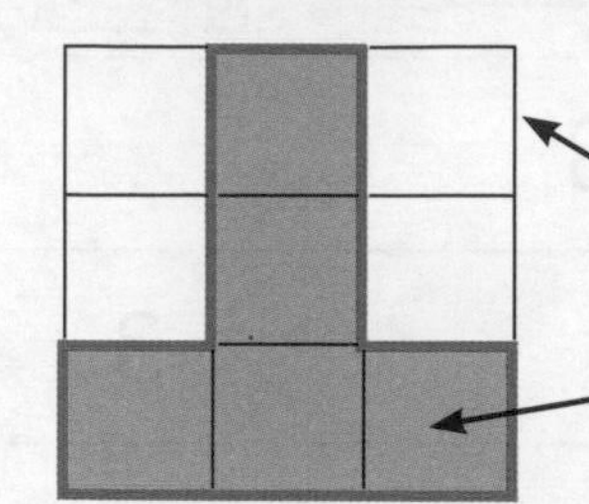

The side of each square is 1 cm, and each square's area is 1 cm^2.

The perimeter of this shape is 12 cm and the area is 5 cm^2.

Now Try These

1. Work out the perimeter and area of the shapes below.

a)

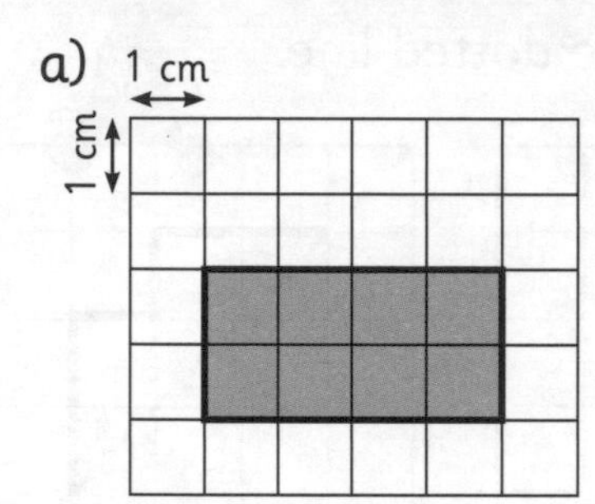

Perimeter = ☐ cm

Area = ☐ cm^2

b)

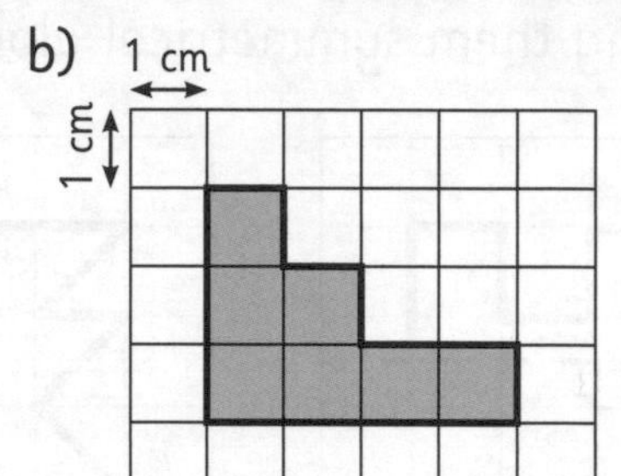

Perimeter = ☐ cm

Area = ☐ cm^2

c)

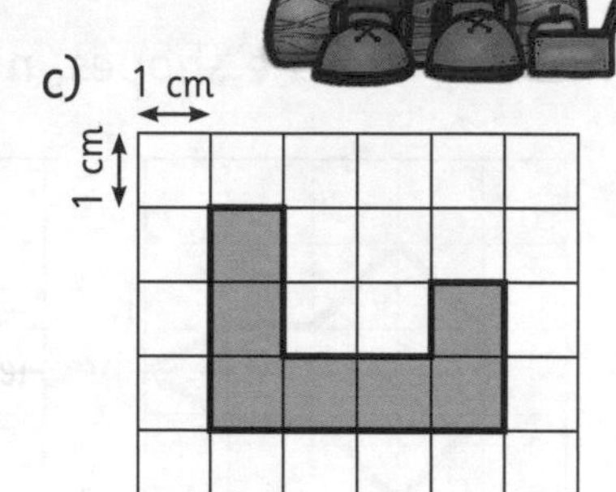

Perimeter = ☐ cm

Area = ☐ cm^2

2. Draw lines to join each rectangle to the leaf showing its perimeter.

3. Work out the shaded area of the shapes below.

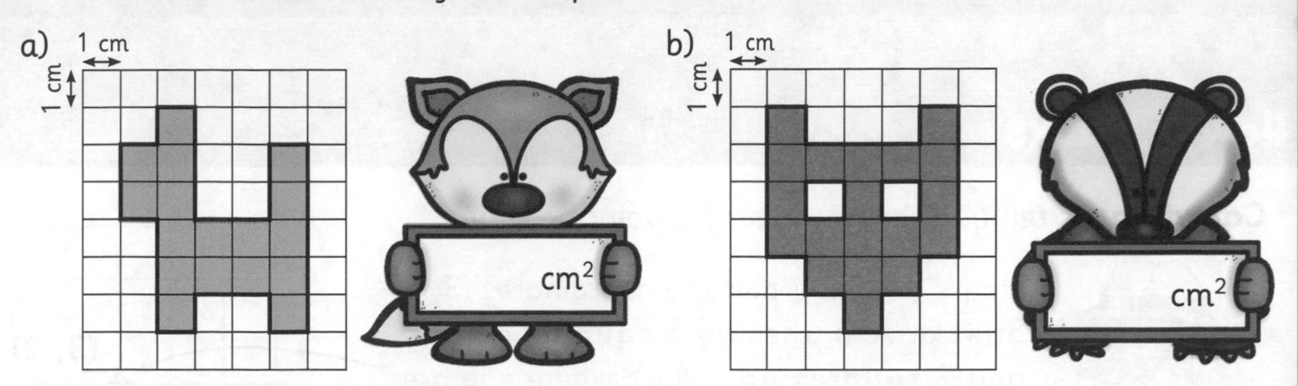

4. Work the perimeter of these shapes.

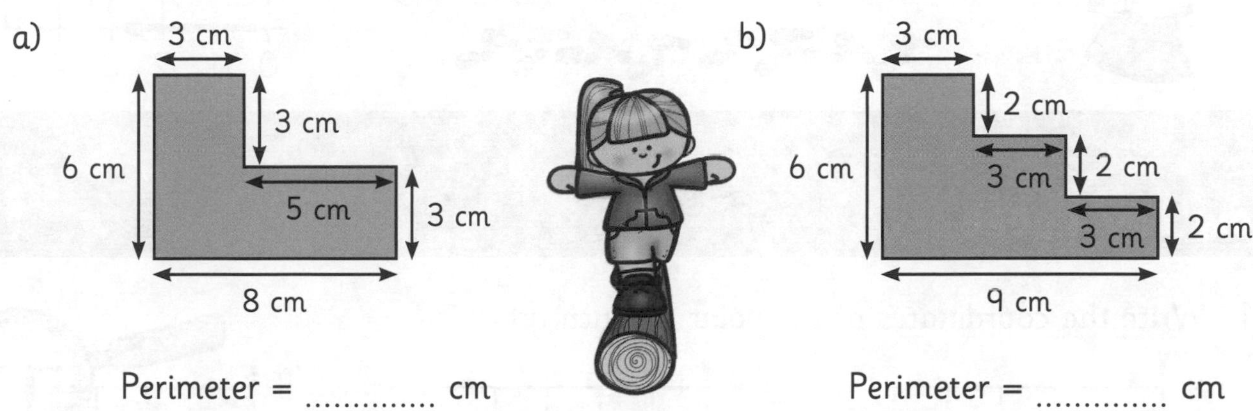

Perimeter = ... cm

Perimeter = ... cm

5. Adil finds a flat square-shaped leaf.
Is has side lengths of 3 cm.
Work out the area of the leaf.

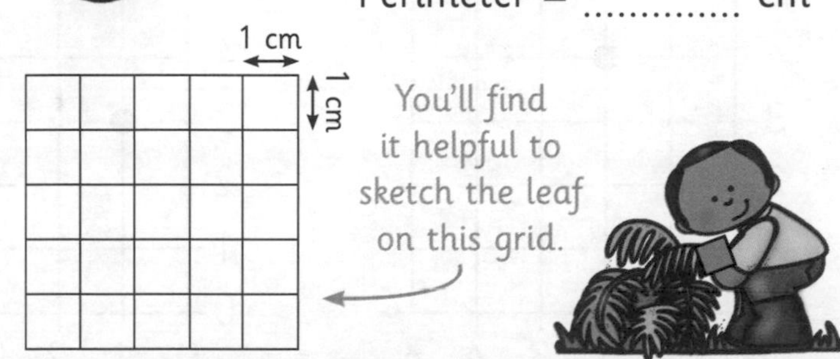

Area = ... cm²

An Extra Challenge

A park ranger is putting up a fence around a picnic site.
He's made these notes about the shape and size of the site:

Shape:	Rectangle
Width:	36 m
Length:	42 m

What is the total length of fence that is needed to surround the picnic site?

How was that? Is this an area you need to improve on?

Coordinates

How It Works

Coordinates tell you the position of a point on a grid.

Here's how you plot the coordinates (**3**, **2**):
Start at zero, then go **3 squares across** and **2 squares up**. Mark where you are.

Always count **across** first, and then **up**.

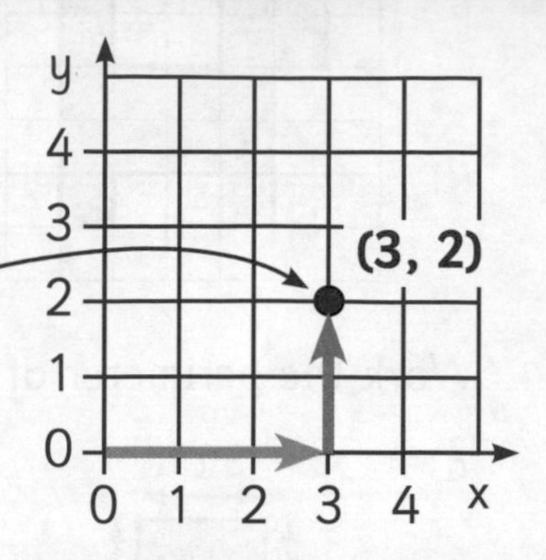

Now Try These

1. Write the coordinates of the point on each grid.

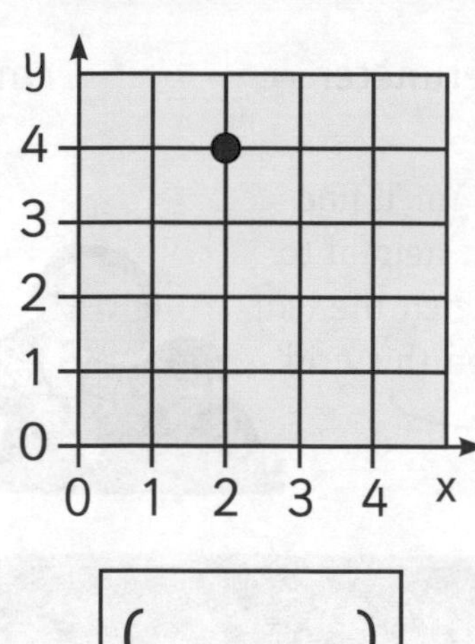

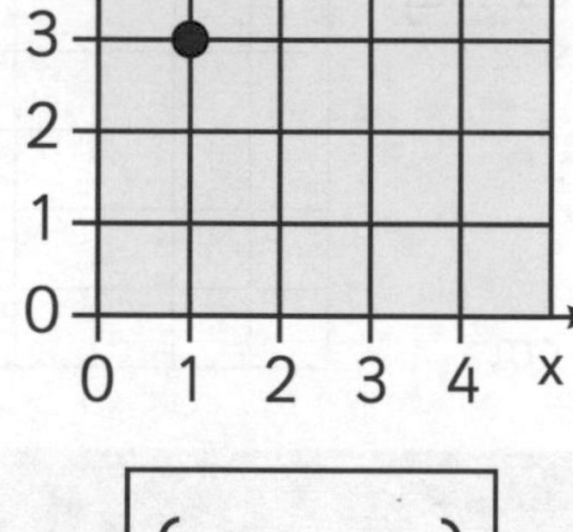

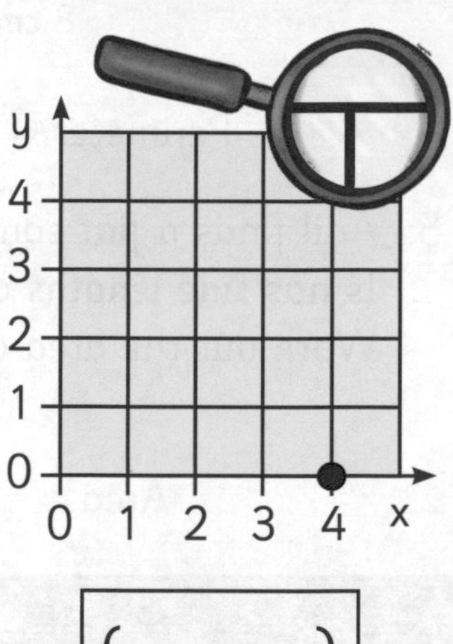

(,)   (,)   (,)

2. Detective Goodboy has sniffed out some clues.

   a) Plot the coordinates of each clue on the grid.

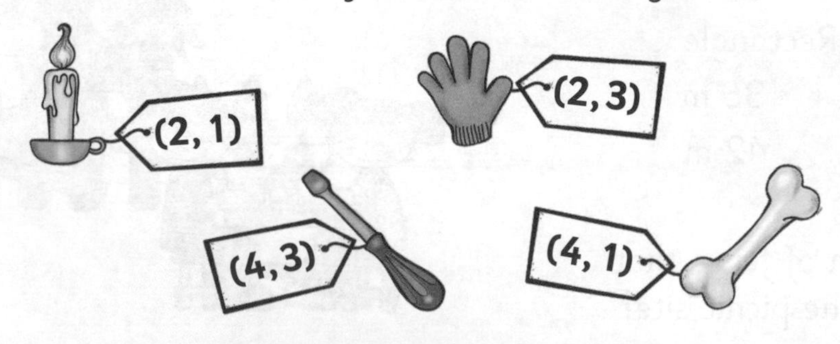

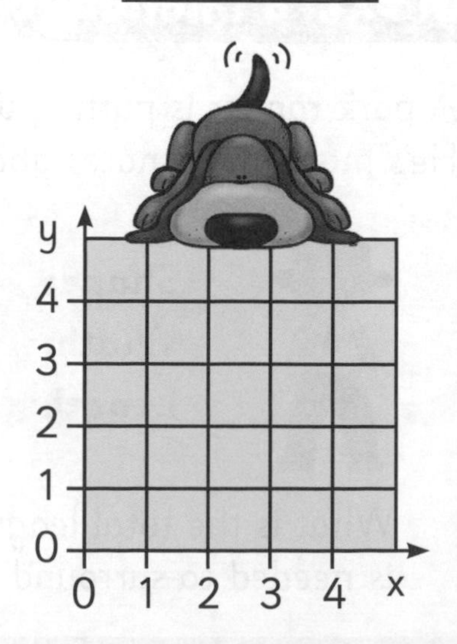

   b) Join up the coordinates to make a shape.
   What shape have you made? ....

3. A suspect has been spotted at the following coordinates.

(0, 2) (1, 3) (3, 3) (4, 2) (2, 0)

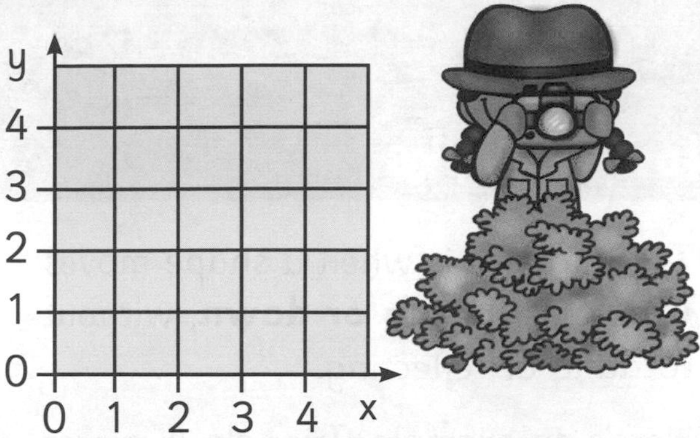

a) Draw the coordinates on the grid and join them up in order.

b) Circle the item below that most closely matches the shape you have drawn.

4. a) Draw the missing point and join it up with the others to make a parallelogram on the grid.

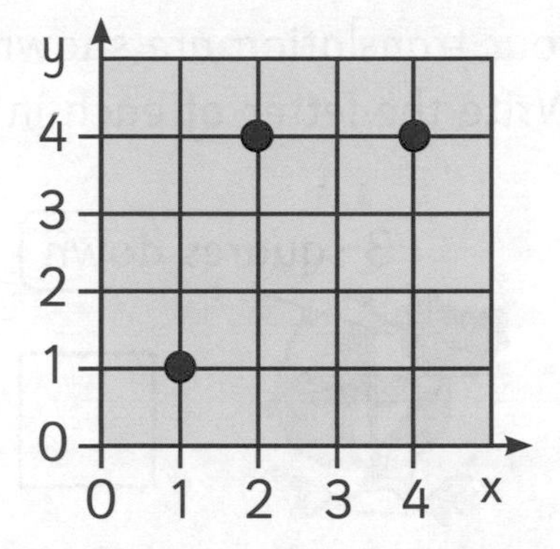

b) What are the coordinates of the point that you've drawn?

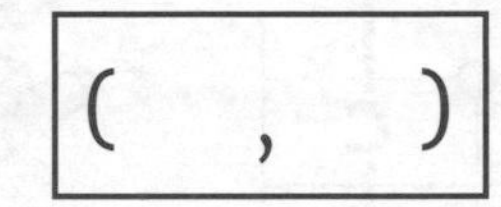

An Extra Challenge

You've almost cracked the case. You just need to name the culprit.
Write down the letters at the following coordinates to work it out.

(4, 4) (5, 2) (3, 1) (1, 5) (4, 2)
(4, 5) (5, 5) (5, 2) (5, 5) (3, 5) (5, 2)
(4, 4) (2, 1) (5, 5)
(2, 4) (5, 3) (5, 3) (4, 5)
(2, 5) (5, 3) (5, 1)

TOP SECRET

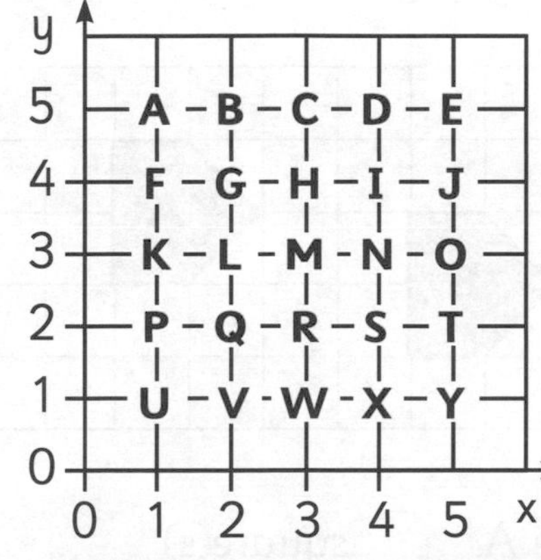

How did it go? Did you solve these problems?

Translation

How It Works

Translation is when a shape moves **left or right**, **up or down**, without rotating or reflecting.

Here's an example: Triangle A moves **4 squares right** and **1 square down** to get to Triangle B.

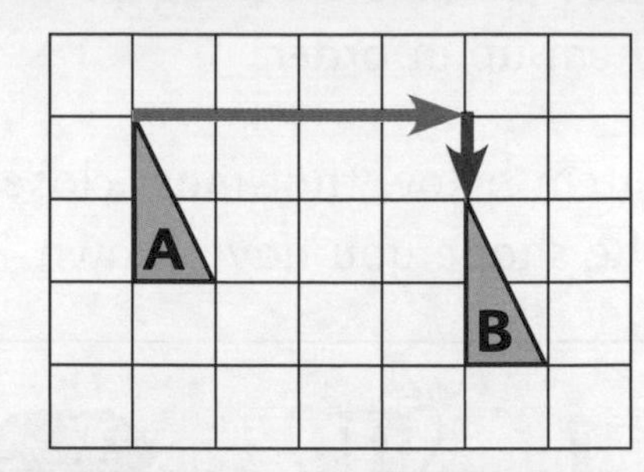

Now Try These

1. Four translation are shown on the grid below.
   Write the letter of each in the box below its description.

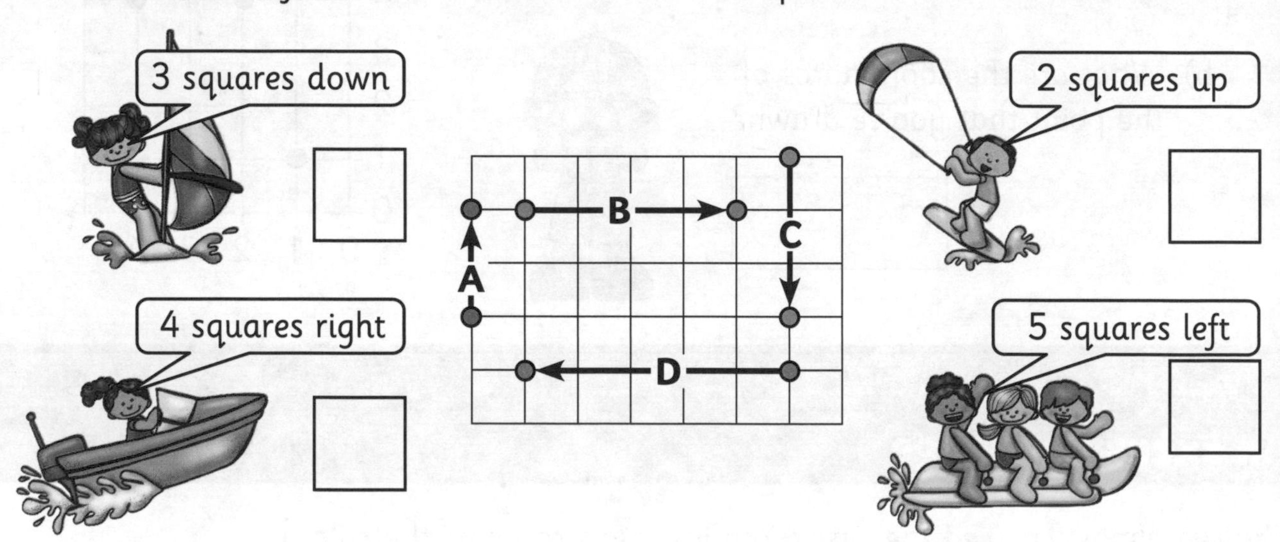

2. Fill in the gaps to describe each translation from shape A to shape B.

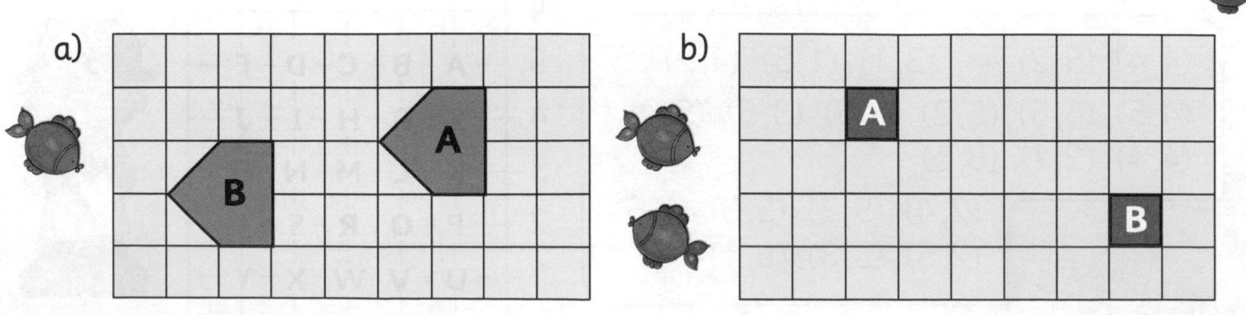

a) Move A .... square(s) .... and .... square(s) ....

b) Move A .... square(s) .... and .... square(s) ....

3. Tick (✔) or cross (✘) each box to say whether each diagram shows a translation.

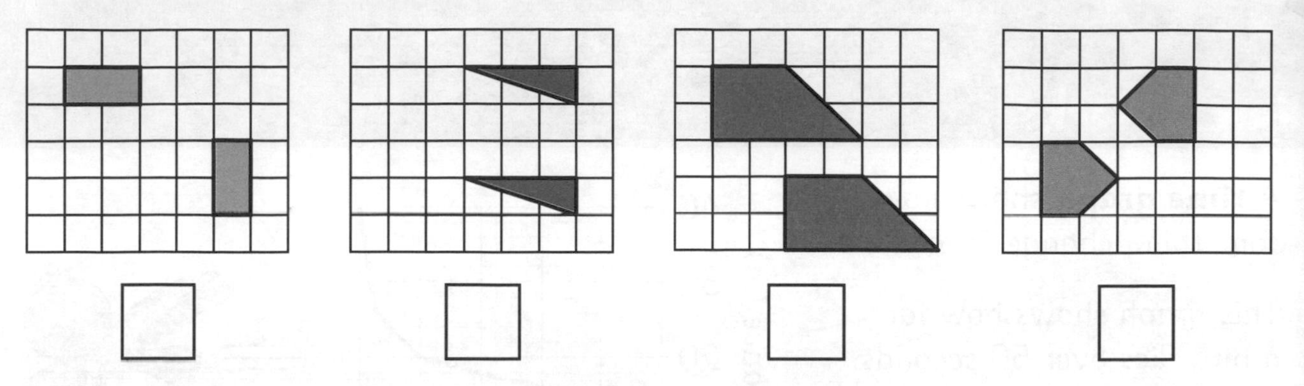

4. Draw the translations of the four shapes (A-D) below.
Colour each new shape to match the original shape.

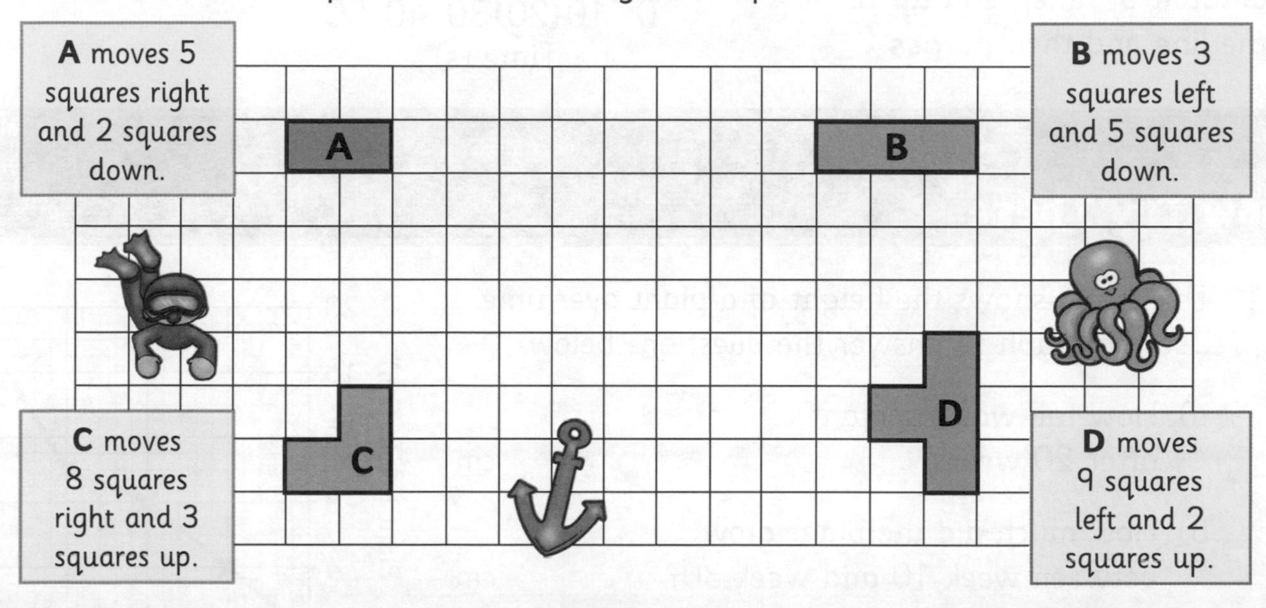

An Extra Challenge

Look again at the shapes A-D from Question 4.

Describe a translation of shapes A, C and D (on the same grid) so that the translated shapes join together with shape B to form the larger shape below.

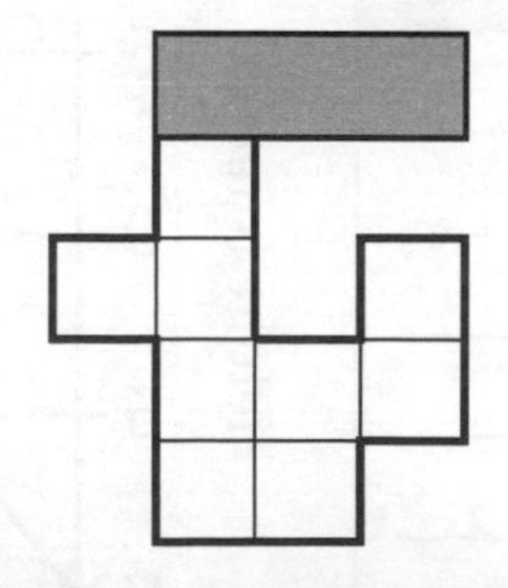

How did you do?
Were translations any trouble?

Charts and Graphs

How It Works

A **time graph** shows how something changes over time.

This graph shows how far a bird flies over 50 seconds.

To see how far the bird has flown after a certain amount of time, read **up** to the line and then **across**.

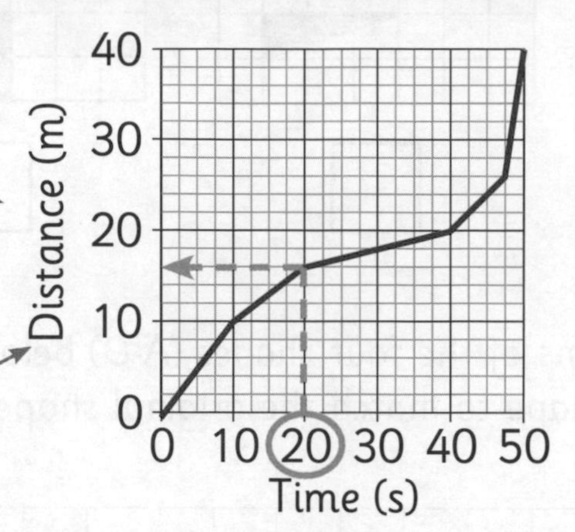

After **20 s**, the bird has flown **16 m**.

Now Try These

1. The graph shows the height of a plant over time. Use the graph to answer the questions below.

   a) How tall was the plant after 20 weeks? .... cm

   b) How much did the plant grow between week 10 and week 30? .... cm

   c) After how many weeks was the plant 18 cm tall? .... weeks

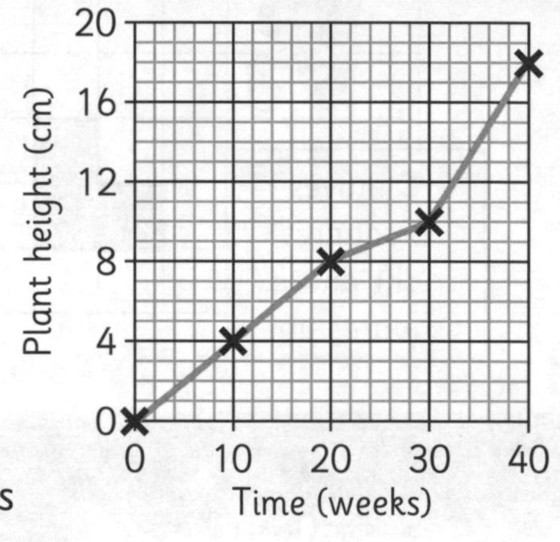

2. Nicola releases a balloon and records its height in a table. Plot the points in the table on the graph and join them up with straight lines.

Time (minutes)	Height (metres)
0	0
5	6
10	12
15	13
20	16
25	16
30	19

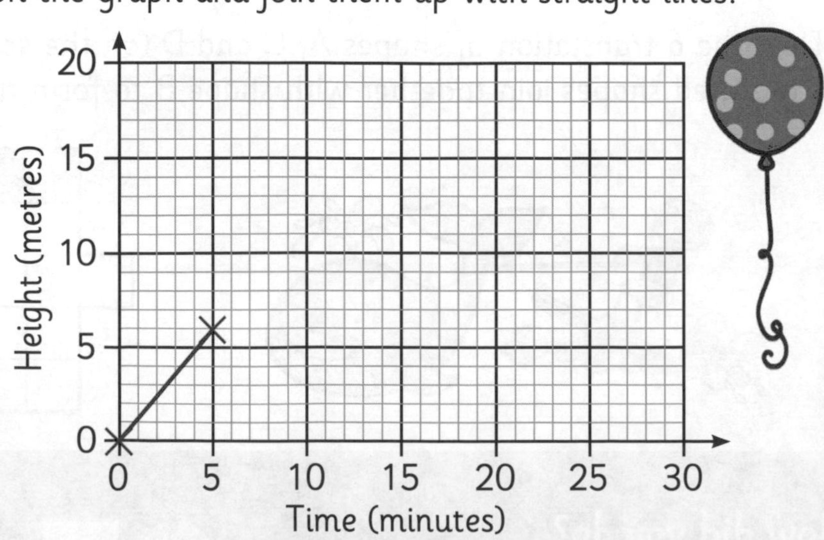

3. Anwar let a frog loose in his school. This bar chart shows how many times the frog was seen each day.

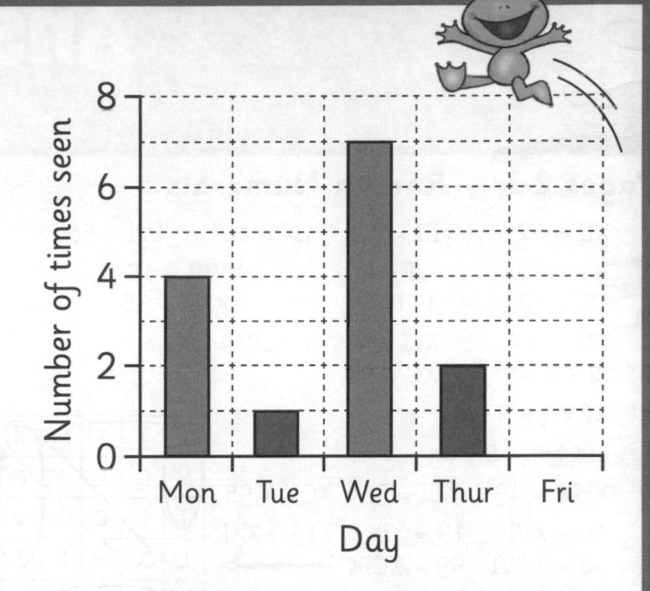

   a) How many times was the frog seen on Monday? ....

   b) How many times was the frog seen on Tuesday and Wednesday in total? ....

   c) The frog was seen 5 times on Friday. Add this data to the bar chart.

4. The pictogram shows the number of birds that Chelsea has seen in her garden over 4 hours.

Hour 1	
Hour 2	
Hour 3	
Hour 4	

   a) How many birds did she see in Hour 2? ....

   b) How many fewer birds did she see in Hour 3 than in Hour 4? ....

   c) How many birds did she see in total? ....

An Extra Challenge

The graph below shows the results of a bouncing competition.

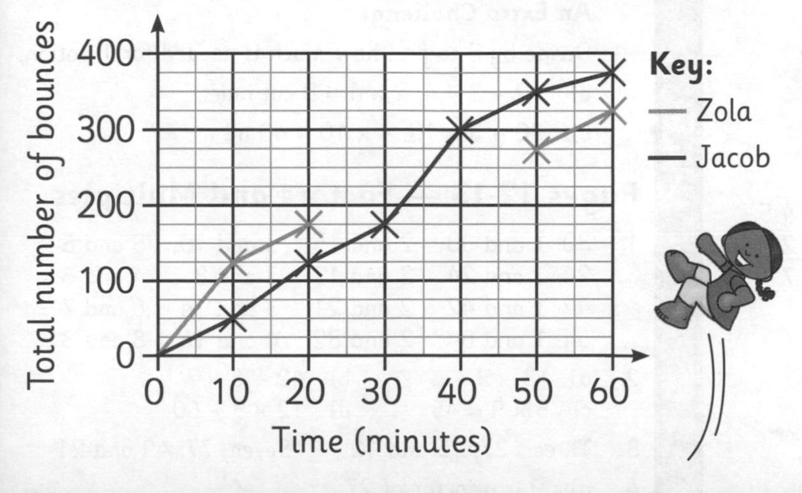

Zola's graph is missing two points. Use the information below to complete her graph.

- At 30 minutes, Zola had bounced 50 more times than Jacob.
- She then took a 10 minute break before continuing to bounce.

How was that? Did you have a tough time with charts?

Answers

Pages 2-3 — Roman Numerals

1. XII = 12 VIII = 8 LX = 60 LVI = 56
2. XX = 20 VI = 6 XVIII = 18
   LII = 52 LXI = 61 XXXV = 35
3. XIV = 14 XLI = 41 LIV = 54
   XLV = 45 XC = 90
4. XCVII = 97
5. LIX km = 59 km
6. XLIX = 49 XCI = 91 XCV = 95
7. 16 = XVI 19 = XIX 71 = LXXI
   96 = XCVI 99 = XCIX →

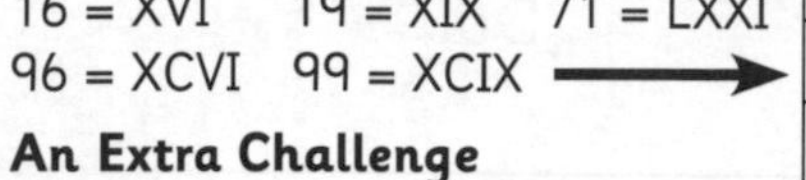

X	I	X	M	X
V	D	L	I	C
I	L	C	D	V
L	X	M	L	I
M	L	X	X	I

An Extra Challenge

a) XLVII = 47

b) Next year Albus will be 48 = XLVIII, so no he can't.

c) The largest number you can make is LXVII = 67.

Pages 4-5 — Decimals

1. 7.**3**4: 3 tenths 4.7**3**: 3 hundredths **3**.47: 3 ones
2. 1.4<u>5</u>: Five hundredths <u>4</u>.32: Four ones
   0.<u>9</u>6: Nine tenths 2.0<u>6</u>: Six hundredths
3. 1.9 4.0 1.02
4. 3.12 3.23 3.28 3.80 3.81
5. Emperor, Patriot, Keith, Monarch
6. 2.30 1.91 1.01 0.95

An Extra Challenge

a) 1.<u>3</u>8 has 3 tenths. Take away 2 tenths to find he was 1.<u>1</u>8 metres the last time he was measured.

b) 1.3<u>8</u> has 8 hundredths. Take away 3 hundredths to find Gaz is 1.3<u>5</u> metres tall without his shoes.

Pages 6-7 — Written Addition

1. 219 + 62 = 281 (carry 1)
   124 + 615 = 739
   253 + 564 = 817 (carry 1)
   3716 + 48 = 3764 (carry 1)
   5326 + 344 = 5670 (carry 1)
   7559 + 1064 = 8623 (carries 1 1)
2. 1348 + 645 = 1993 m (carry 1)
3. 32.3 + 37.6 = 69.9
4. 2.45 + 1.29 = £ 3.74 (carry 1)
5. a) 24.7 + 72.4 = 97.1 g (carry 1)
   b) 268.5 + 323.7 = 592.2 ml (carries 1 1)

An Extra Challenge

2.48 + 7.34 = 9.82 (carry 1)

8.04 + 11.93 = 19.97

Pages 8-9 — Written Subtraction

1. 4758 − 231 = 4527
   5895 − 4621 = 1274
   6782 (exchanged: 5 17 7 12) − 866 = 5916
2. 4131 (exchanged: 2 11) − 107 = 4024
3. 9542 (exchanged: 4 14) − 3281 = 6261
4. a) 1835 (exchanged: 7 13) − 542 = 1293
   b) 1835 (exchanged: 0 18 2 15) − 919 = 916
5. 26.8 − 2.1 = 24.7
   27.97 (exchanged: 8 17) − 13.88 = 14.09
   51.32 (exchanged: 4 10 10 13) − 34.40 = 16.92
6. 1.09 (exchanged: 0 10) − 0.54 = 0.55 litres

An Extra Challenge

For example:

5.00 (exchanged: 4 9 10 10) − 1.54 = 3.46 → 3.46 (exchanged: 2 14) − 1.93 = 1.53 → 1.53 (exchanged: 4 13) − 1.16 = 0.37

So Janette has £0.37 (37p) left over.

Pages 10-11 — Times Tables

1. 3 × 9 = 27 2 × 12 = 24 3 × 1 = 3
   8 × 11 = 88 10 × 4 = 40 6 × 0 = 0
2. 8 × 7 = 56
3. 3 × 11 = 33
4. 6 × 12 = 72
5. 9 × 7 = 63
6. 81 ÷ 9 = 9 28 ÷ 7 = 4 12 ÷ 1 = 12
   5 ÷ 5 = 1 22 ÷ 2 = 11 48 ÷ 6 = 8
7. 35 ÷ 7 = 5
8. 48 ÷ 4 = 12
9. a) 7 × 3 = 21 b) 6 × 11 = 66
   c) 3 × 4 × 5 = 60 d) 2 × 6 × 3 = 36

An Extra Challenge

Divide by 3 to find how much is needed for 1 potion.

a) 12 ÷ 3 = 4, 2 × 4 = 8 cat hairs

b) 30 ÷ 3 = 10, 4 × 10 = 40 ml

Pages 12-13 — Factors and Multiples

1. 30: 1 and 30 2 and 15 3 and 10 5 and 6
   24: 1 and 24 2 and 12 3 and 8 4 and 6
   42: 1 and 42 2 and 21 3 and 14 6 and 7
   64: 1 and 64 2 and 32 4 and 16 8 and 8
2. a) 18 ÷ 3 = 6 b) 42 ÷ 6 = 7
   c) 5 × 9 = 45 d) 12 × 5 = 60
3. Three: 27, 15 and 12 Seven: 77, 49 and 21
4. a) 9 is a factor of 27. ✔
   b) 16 is a multiple of 3. ✘
   c) 4 is a factor of 34. ✘
   d) 72 is a multiple of 8. ✔

Answers

An Extra Challenge

a) $4 \times 9 = 36$

b) $2 \times 3 = 6$, $2 \times 9 = 18$, $4 \times 3 = 12$, $4 \times 9 = 36$

Pages 14-15 — Written Multiplication

1. John:

$$\begin{array}{r} 26 \\ \times\ \ 3 \\ \hline 18 \\ 60 \\ \hline 78 \end{array}$$

Penny:

$$\begin{array}{r} 32 \\ \times\ \ 4 \\ \hline 8 \\ 120 \\ \hline 128 \end{array}$$

Osita:

$$\begin{array}{r} 45 \\ \times\ \ 8 \\ \hline 40 \\ 320 \\ \hline 360 \end{array}$$

Tahel:

$$\begin{array}{r} 58 \\ \times\ \ 8 \\ \hline 64 \\ 400 \\ \hline 464 \end{array}$$

2.

$$\begin{array}{r} 14 \\ \times\ \ 8 \\ \hline 32 \\ 80 \\ \hline 112 \end{array}$$

3.

$$\begin{array}{r} 36 \\ \times\ \ 7 \\ \hline 42 \\ 210 \\ \hline 252 \end{array}$$

4. a)

$$\begin{array}{r} 350 \\ \times\ \ 4 \\ \hline 0 \\ 200 \\ 1200 \\ \hline 1400 \end{array}$$

b)

$$\begin{array}{r} 203 \\ \times\ \ 4 \\ \hline 12 \\ 0 \\ 800 \\ \hline 812 \end{array}$$

c)

$$\begin{array}{r} 916 \\ \times\ \ 6 \\ \hline 36 \\ 60 \\ 5400 \\ \hline 5496 \end{array}$$

d)

$$\begin{array}{r} 783 \\ \times\ \ 3 \\ \hline 9 \\ 240 \\ 2100 \\ \hline 2349 \end{array}$$

An Extra Challenge

You need to work out:

$$\begin{array}{r} 13 \\ \times\ \ 6 \\ \hline 18 \\ 60 \\ \hline 78 \end{array} \rightarrow \begin{array}{r} 78 \\ \times\ \ 7 \\ \hline 56 \\ 490 \\ \hline 546 \end{array} \rightarrow \begin{array}{r} 546 \\ \times\ \ 9 \\ \hline 54 \\ 360 \\ 4500 \\ \hline 4914 \end{array}$$

So the stone monument is 4914 years old.

Pages 16-17 — Fractions 1

1. a) $22 \div 2 = 11$ b) $12 \div 3 = 4$, $4 \times 2 = 8$
   c) $40 \div 8 = 5$, $5 \times 3 = 15$
   d) $18 \div 6 = 3$, $3 \times 5 = 15$
2. E.g.

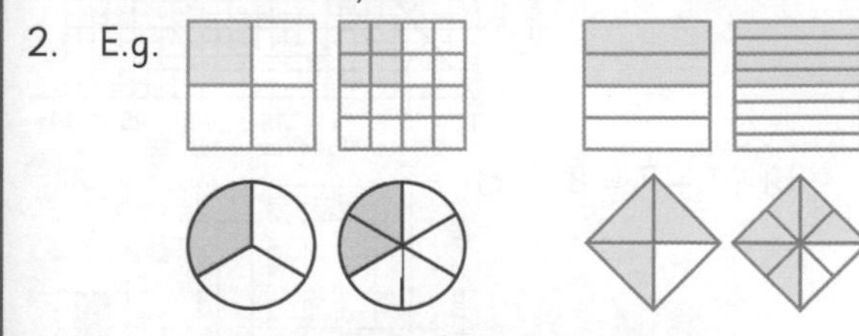

3. a) $15 \div 5 = 3$, $3 \times 2 = 6$ slices
   b) $42 \div 7 = 6$, $6 \times 4 = 24$ mushrooms slices
4. $= \frac{4}{6}$ $= \frac{2}{3}$ $= \frac{8}{12}$
5. $56 \div 8 = 7$, $7 \times 3 = 21$ m
6. a) $\frac{10}{100} = \frac{1}{10}$ b) $\frac{40}{100} = \frac{4}{10}$
7. £100 ÷ 100 = £1, £1 × 29 = £29

An Extra Challenge

a) $15 \div 5 = 3$, $3 \times 3 = 9$, so Kim saves £9.

b) $15 \div 3 = 5$, $5 \times 2 = 10$, so Leo saves £10.
Kim saves less than Leo, so Kim will pay more.

Pages 18-19 — Around the World

The Arctic: 24 → Europe: 34 → Asia: 30 → Antarctica: 20 → Australia: 30 → Africa: 7 → North America: 3 → South America: 2 → The Arctic

Pages 20-21 — Fractions 2

1. $0.8 = \frac{8}{10}$ $0.47 = \frac{47}{100}$ $0.05 = \frac{5}{100}$
2. $\frac{1}{3} + \frac{1}{3} = \frac{2}{3}$ $\frac{4}{10} + \frac{3}{10} = \frac{7}{10}$ $\frac{3}{8} + \frac{4}{8} = \frac{7}{8}$
3. a) $\frac{2}{4}$ (or $\frac{1}{2}$), 0.5 b) $\frac{4}{10}$ (or $\frac{2}{5}$), 0.4
4. a) $\frac{2}{9}$ b) $\frac{5}{8}$ c) $\frac{1}{11}$
5. a) $\frac{1}{100}$ b) $\frac{17}{100}$
6. $\frac{7}{10} = 0.7$ $\frac{82}{100} = 0.82$ $\frac{29}{100} = 0.29$

An Extra Challenge

$\frac{\mathbf{4}}{10} + \frac{5}{10} = 0.9$ $\frac{3}{10} + \frac{\mathbf{3}}{10} = 0.6$

$\frac{4}{100} - \frac{\mathbf{2}}{100} = 0.02$ $\frac{22}{100} - \frac{\mathbf{5}}{100} = 0.17$

Pages 22-23 — Rounding

1. 731: 730 700 1000
   1069: 1070 1100 1000
2. 1.2 → 1 5.2 → 5 7.8 → 8
3. 329, 328, 327, 330, 331
4. a) $30 + 20 = 50$ b) $60 - 50 = 10$
5. $1.9 + 5.2 \rightarrow 2 + 5 = 7$ $12.4 - 4.7 \rightarrow 12 - 5 = 7$
   $3.3 \times 5.1 \rightarrow 3 \times 5 = 15$

An Extra Challenge

a) Yes — 97 = 100 to the nearest 10.

b) 95 days — as 95 is the smallest number that rounds up to 100 to the nearest 10.

c) 104 days — as 104 is the largest number that rounds down to 100 to the nearest 10.

Pages 24-25 — Problem Solving

1.

$$\begin{array}{r} \overset{11\ \ 10}{\not{1}\not{2}0} \\ -\ \ 57 \\ \hline 63 \end{array} \qquad \begin{array}{r} 63 \\ +\ \ 91 \\ \hline 154 \end{array}$$

1st: Abigail — 154 points
2nd: Winona — 120 points
3rd: Claire — 63 points

2.

$$\begin{array}{r} \overset{10\ \ 12}{\not{1}\not{1}2} \\ -\ \ 64 \\ \hline 48 \end{array} \qquad \begin{array}{r} 48 \\ +\ \ 37 \\ \hline 85 \\ {\scriptstyle 1} \end{array}$$

So Ruth has 85 eggs.

3.

$$\begin{array}{r} 14 \\ \times\ \ 6 \\ \hline 24 \\ 60 \\ \hline 84 \end{array}$$

Martin scores 84 points in the first 6 events. He scores $3 \times 7 = 21$ points in the remaining events. So Martin scores $84 + 21 = 105$ points in total.

4. Under 10s total: 15 × £5 = £75
   11-16 year olds total: £159 – £75 = £84
   So £84 ÷ £7 = 12 members are 11-16 years old.

Answers

5. 3 × 50p = £1.50, so it's cheaper for James to buy as many packs of 3 as possible.

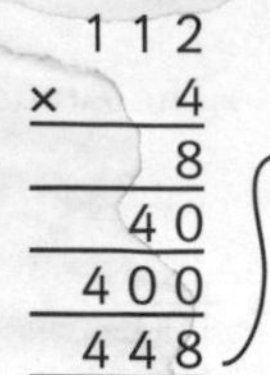

So James can buy 4 packs of 3 bottles for £4.48. He has £5 – £4.48 = 52p left over, so he can also buy one more bottle for 50p. Then he will get 2p in change.

An Extra Challenge

Jessica and Peter ran 240 m – 60 m = 180 m in total.
80 m + 100 m = 180 m and 100 m – 80 m = 20 m.
So Peter ran 80 m.

Pages 26-27 — Shapes and Angles

1. a) '**equilateral**' is the correct word
   b) '**kite**' is the correct word

2. regular hexagon, scalene triangle, equilateral triangle, irregular hexagon

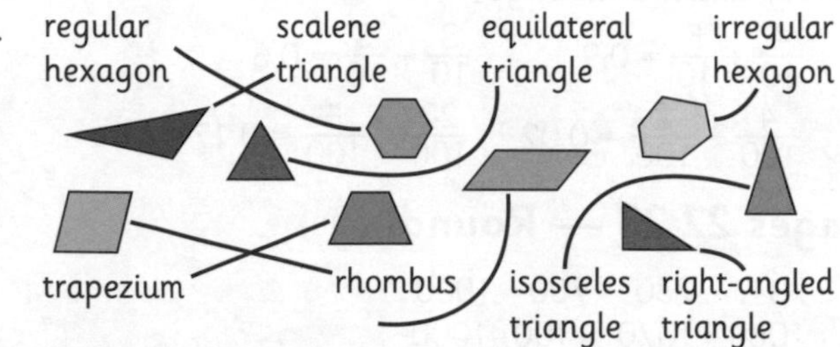

trapezium, rhombus, isosceles triangle, right-angled triangle

3.

Number of sides	3	5	6
Number of acute angles	3	3	2
Number of obtuse angles	0	2	4
Number of lines of symmetry	3	1	2

4.

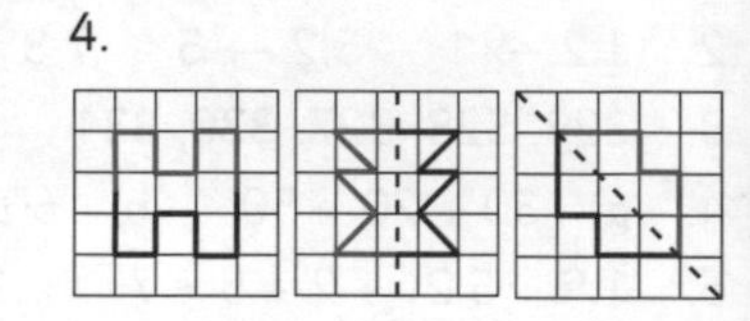

An Extra Challenge

"It has three angles..." — it's a **right-angled triangle**.
"It has five sides..." — it's a **regular pentagon**.
"It's a quadrilateral..." — it's a **rhombus**.

Pages 28-29 — Perimeter and Area

1. a) Perimeter = 12 cm Area = 8 cm^2
   b) Perimeter = 14 cm Area = 7 cm^2
   c) Perimeter = 16 cm Area = 7 cm^2

2. 3 m by 3 m : 12 m 4 m by 4 m : 16 m
   7 m by 4 m : 22 m 3 m by 9 m : 24 m
   2 m by 5 m : 14 m 4 m by 5 m : 18 m

3. a) 17 cm^2 b) 19 cm^2

4. a) 28 cm b) 30 cm 5. 9 cm^2

An Extra Challenge

Length of fence = perimeter of site
= 36 + 42 + 36 + 42 = 156 m

Pages 30-31 — Coordinates

1. (2,4) (1,3) (4,0)

2. a) b) Square

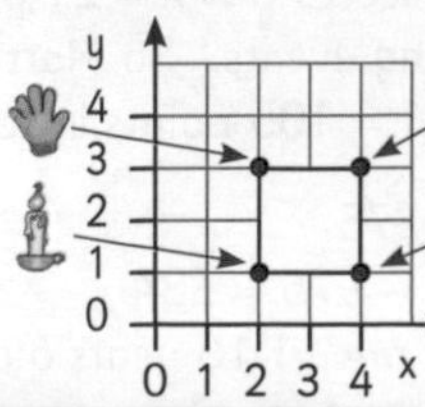

3. a) b)

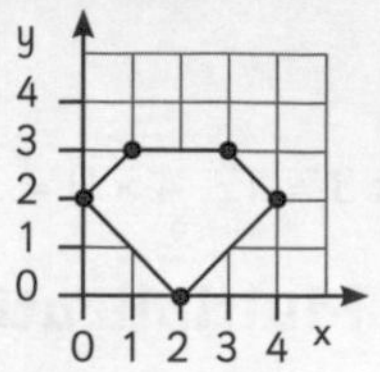

An Extra Challenge

IT WAS DETECTIVE GOODBOY

4. a)

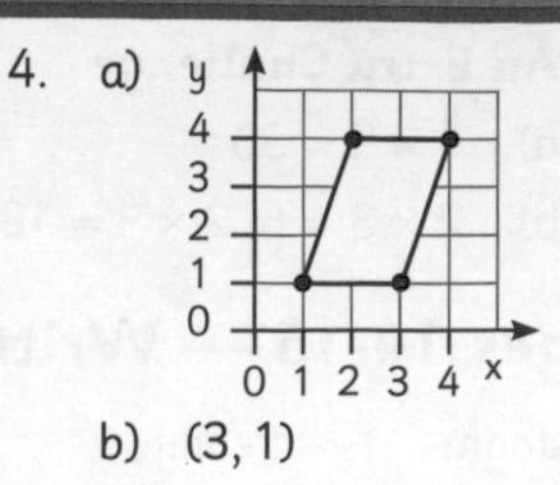

b) (3, 1)

Pages 32-33 — Translation

1. 3 squares down — C 2 squares up — A
   4 squares right — B 5 squares left — D

2. a) Move **4** squares **left** and **1** square **down**.
   b) Move **5** squares **right** and **2** squares **down**.

3.

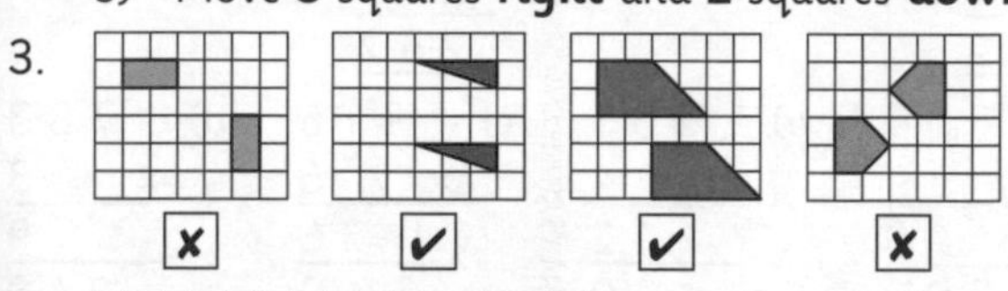

✗ ✓ ✓ ✗

4.

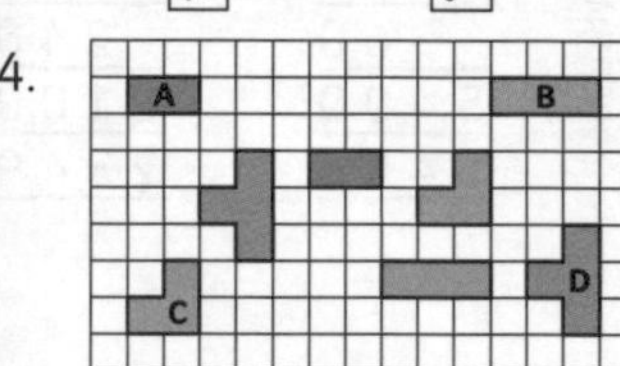

An Extra Challenge

A: 10 squares right and 4 squares down
C: 11 squares right and 3 squares up
D: 2 squares left and 3 squares up

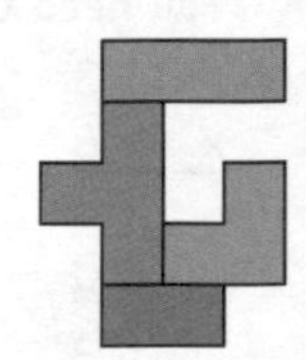

Pages 34-35 — Charts and Graphs

1. a) 8 cm
   b) 10 – 4 = 6 cm
   c) 40 weeks

2.

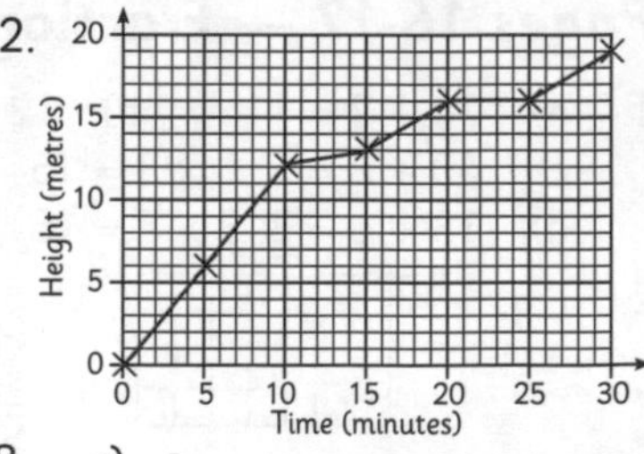

3. a) 4 b) 1 + 7 = 8 c)

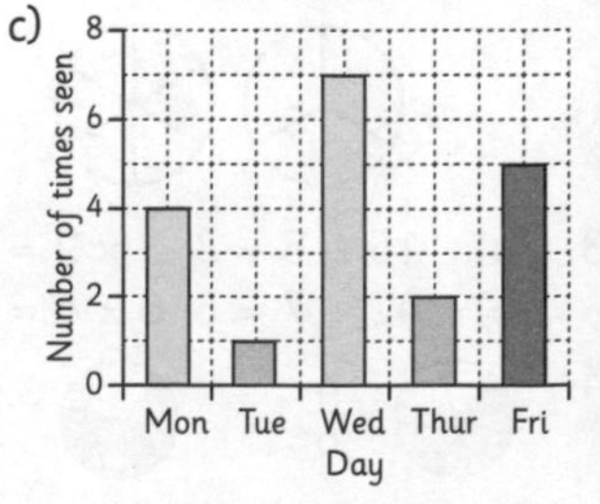

4. a) 3 b) 5 – 1 = 4
   c) 4 + 3 + 1 + 5 = 13

An Extra Challenge

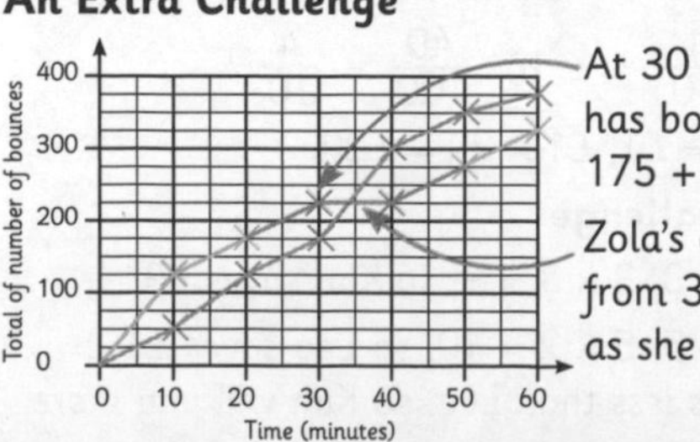

At 30 minutes, Zola has bounced a total of 175 + 50 = 225 times.

Zola's graph is flat from 30 to 40 minutes as she took a break.